THE ART OF THE RECITATION OF THE QUR'ĀN

TAJWĪD

THE ART OF THE RECITATION OF THE QUR'ĀN

TAJWĪD

ABDUL MAJID KHAN

TUGHRA
BOOKS
New Jersey

16 15 14 13   1 2 3 4

Published by Tughra Books
345 Clifton Ave., Clifton,
NJ, 07011, USA

www.tughrabooks.com

Library of Congress Cataloging-in-Publication Data Available

ISBN: 978-1-59784-318-8

Printed by
Çağlayan A.Ş., Izmir - Turkey

Contents

Chapter One
INTRODUCTION TO TAJWĪD

Chapter Two
REVIEW OF ARABIC

Chapter Three
PHONETICS

Chapter Four
THE RULES OF TAJWĪD

Chapter Five

THE RULES OF RECITATION

Chapter Six

MOST COMMON ERRORS

Chapter Seven

MANNERS OF RECITATION

List of Tables

List of Charts

List of Figures

DEDICATION

TO YOU, O ALMIGHTY ALLAH!

WITHOUT YOUR GUIDANCE AND HELP

THIS WORK COULD NEVER HAVE BEEN COMPLETED

AND

TO THE BELOVED AND FINAL MESSENGER OF ALLAH:

MUHAMMAD ﷺ

IT WAS THROUGH HIM THAT THE QUR'AN WAS GIVEN

TO HUMANKIND.

ACKNOWLEDGMENTS

My deepest thanks to my wife, Kausar, and to my three daughters, Ayesha, Nadia, and Saadia. All of them gave up so much of my companionship so that I could complete the work.

I am intellectually and spiritually indebted to my father, Mohammad Abdul Aleem Khan, Chairman and Director of the Islamic Center of Corona, New York, and to my mother, Farooqa Begum, who has held weekly gatherings in Pakistan and New York for the last thirty five years. Their teachings about Islam have been a continued source of spiritual inspiration and provided me a solid intellectual and educational base.

My thanks to Sheikh Shukrallah El-Nour of Sudan for his review of material and suggestions for improvements. Again, I am thankful to Alauddin Khalid of the Urdu Academy Sindh, Karachi, for his technical assistance, and to my dearest friend and neighbor, Dr. Muzammil Siddiqi, who entrusted me to run the Weekend Islamic School for children in Teaneck, New Jersey, U.S.A. This opportunity brought me very close to young minds eager to learn and to live a life according to the teachings of our great religion. It was there that I learned that the traditional teaching methods of Islamic education used in most eastern countries were not suitable to teach our children born in the West. Along with audio-visual methods, I prepared the course material, combining the text with graphic arts to enhance their learning. This book is based on the teaching methods derived from that valuable experience.

Special thanks are expressed to the staff editors of the Tughra Books for their astute corrections and editing. Last but not least, my deepest thanks to all of them who typed manuscripts many times over. My special thanks to İbrahim Akdağ, Serdar Aşlar and Hüseyin Kasımoğlu who typed and retyped the manuscript with great patience, a sense of personal pride, and commitment. May Allah the Almighty reward all of them. Āmīn!

PREFACE

The Qur'an is the Speech of Allah and His last revelation that has been sent to all of humanity. We should, therefore, give its recitation its just due by reading it according to the rules and principles of the art of Qur'anic recitation. When it is recited distinctly in a slow, rhythmic, and enchanted fashion, with proper pauses and stops, and the correct rise and fall of the reader's voice, the great effect of the Divine words penetrates the mind and the soul. It descends into the heart and becomes firmly set therein. For the sake of understanding the Qur'an, it is highly recommended to recite it distinctly, with both the mind and heart concentrated on it. As for others, it is recommended for the non-Arabic speaking Muslims who do not understand its meanings to recite it distinctly, since this is closer to respect, and has much more impact on the heart. It is also to be noted that the knowledge of *Tajwīd*, or the art of the recitation of the Qur'an, will surely help readers in achieving the ultimate goal of understanding the Message of the Qur'an.

This book on the art of the recitation of the Holy Qur'an is easy to follow with its simple yet detailed presentation of subjects, and is accessible to beginners who have had little exposure to Tajwīd. This work provides both the young and adult English speaking Muslims with the best organization and presentation of the art of Tajwīd, and is done in a beautiful and fascinating printing.

It is said that the art of Tajwīd cannot be mastered without a teacher. This is true. However, not all of us have time to go to a *qāri'*, who is an expert on Tajwīd, or a qāri' is simply not available in many cities of the English speaking world. For this reason, in addition to the description and examples, I have included charts, tables, figures and summaries. The intention is to give readers a different view of the subject under discussion. This will provide some remedy for not having a teacher. Again, one cannot master the art of Tajwīd from the theoretical knowledge alone unless it is followed by daily practice in recitation of the Qur'an.

PREREQUISITES FOR THIS BOOK

This book is primarily intended for English speaking Muslims living in Western countries. Those who know English as a second language can also equally benefit from it.

It presupposes the usual ability to read the Qur'anic text. It does not require any knowledge of the Arabic grammar or understanding of the Arabic language. That said, it will certainly be helpful if one is familiar with Arabic grammar or can understand Arabic language.

Although a user is required to be able to read Arabic, terms such as *ḥaraka* (vowels), *sukūn* (no vowel), *shadda* (double consonant mark), *ghunna* (nasalization), *tanwīn* (double *fatha*, double *ḍamma*, double *kasra*), *hamzatu'l-waṣl* (*hamza* for connecting words) are covered in a basic review. They are not intended to teach the Arabic language. The reader should also review the definitions of Arabic terms and phonetic terms in the Glossary at the end of the book.

A quick glossary of the most frequently used Arabic terms is also included in Chapter Four where the main rules of Tajwīd are covered. The reader should also make every effort to find a native Arabic speaking Muslim friend or someone who knows Tajwīd to help them in the correct pronunciation of the Arabic alphabet.

ORGANIZATION AND PURPOSE OF THE BOOK

This book is arranged in eight chapters. Each chapter contains a heading which provides sections related to the heading of that chapter. For example, Chapter Three's main heading is Phonetics, which covers all related topics on this subject in four sections:

1. Phonetic Description
2. Transliteration
3. The Organs of Speech
4. The Places and Manners of Articulation

This clear scheme throughout the book will allow the readers to quickly find the subject of their interest by glancing at the table of contents. An extreme caution is taken to stay on the topic under discussion and to avoid any digressions into other areas. When a topic is closely related to another one, an appropriate reference is given in the footnotes to find the detailed explanation elsewhere.

A general weakness of all the books of Tajwīd that I have come across is a lack of glossary of Arabic, phonetic, and other technical terms. By adding these to the end of this book, the readers will be able to find the topic of their interest without flipping through the entire book. Every effort is made to keep the readers' convenience in mind and to cater to their needs.

The purpose of writing this book is not to derive any financial or materialistic gains. The real gain and reward is from Allah, Exalted and Mighty is He! As mentioned in the Qur'an, each Prophet said to his people:

﴿وَمَا أَسْأَلُكُمْ عَلَيْهِ مِنْ أَجْرٍ إِنْ أَجْرِيَ إِلاَّ عَلَى رَبِّ الْعَالَمِينَ﴾

No reward do I ask of you for it: my reward is only from the Lord of the worlds. (ash-Shu'arā' 26:109, 127, 145, 164, 180)

If the readers ever find this book in their hands, I will know that Allah the Almighty has accepted this humble service from me.

FOR THE BEGINNERS

The following chapters will provide sufficient knowledge so that beginners will be able to recite the Qur'an correctly:

Chapter One gives an introduction and explains the significance of learning the recitation, along with some of the errors committed by most readers.

Chapter Two provides a brief overview of Arabic terminology, definitions, and important points to bear in mind. This knowledge is essential in understanding the rules presented in the subsequent chapters.

Chapter Three gives the phonetics of Arabic sounds and manner of articulation of Arabic letters. The sounds foreign to English are pointed out and they can only be learned from an expert or from a native speaker. A detailed description of articulation of all Arabic letters is followed by a figure showing where and how they are pronounced. This is followed by an organizational chart, and lastly, a summary of the same is presented in a tabular form. It is strongly hoped that if a reader missed something in the description he may get it from other views.

The transliteration table is presented in this chapter and at the beginning of the book. This will be helpful in pronouncing the words correctly.

Chapter Four is the heart of the Tajwīd. For beginners, the bare minimum for an acceptable recitation are the rules of Nūn Sakīn and Tanwīn, the rules of the letter Lām, and the rules of Madd. Mastering other rules discussed in this chapter can add further beauty to one's recitation.

The rules of stopping and initiation, as well as the punctuation marks, are presented in Chapter Five. These are essential for the correct recitation of the Qur'an. Beginners should also read Chapter Six to avoid most common errors.

Chapter Seven outlines the objective and subjective conditions, and discusses recitational prostrations. The reader will learn different views held by scholars on the manner of the performance of prostration when a verse requiring a *sajda* occurs. Beginners will also find the Glossary of Arabic and Phonetic terms extremely helpful in learning the rules of Tajwīd as well as the pronunciation of Arabic letters.

FOR THE EXPERTS

The experts of Tajwīd will find this book as a handy reference for themselves. It will also be a source of examples on various topics in explaining the rules of Tajwīd to their students. It is to be remembered that certain ideas are beyond the scope of this book and require a separate treatment. This is true for the script of the Qur'an where the rules of Deletion (اَلْحَذْفُ), Addition (اَلزِّيَادَةُ), Substitution (اَلْبَدَلُ), and the seat of Hamza (اَلْهَمْزَةُ) are summarized in the last chapter. An expert can get the complete rules from one of the references listed at the end of the book.

It is highly recommended that one read this book slowly. Reading one chapter at a time will allow the book's lessons to sink into a reader's heart. If one should find anything in this book incorrect, I ask that such mistakes do not spoil the rest of it. If any mistakes are pointed out to me, quoting the page number, I will be glad to correct all errors in the next edition, InshaAllah. If there is something especially pleasing or helpful, please do not forget to pray to Allah the Almighty for my forgiveness.

It is hoped that this book will be an important aid in the correct recitation of the Holy Qur'an and that its resting place will be on the desk, rather than on the shelf.

ON MENTIONING THE NAME OF ALLAH, THE PROPHETS AND THE COMPANIONS

First of all, Islam teaches that the mention of the names of Allah should be followed by such praises as:

Exalted is He!	تَعَالَى
Glorified is He!	سُبْحَانَهُ
Mighty and Great is He!	عَزَّ وَجَلَّ
Great and Exalted is He!	جَلَّ وَعَلَى
Blessed and Exalted is He!	تَبَارَكَ وَتَعَالَى
Glorified and Exalted is He!	سُبْحَانَهُ وَتَعَالَى

Second, Islam also teaches that the mention of the name of any Prophet should be followed by the invoking of blessings, greetings, or peace of Allah. In case of the Last Messenger, Muhammad, the following Qur'anic verse commands the believers to do so:

﴿إِنَّ اللهَ وَمَلاَئِكَتَهُ يُصَلُّونَ عَلَى النَّبِيِّ يَا أَيُّهَا الَّذِينَ آمَنُوا
صَلُّوا عَلَيْهِ وَسَلِّمُوا تَسْلِيمًا﴾

Surely, Allah and His angels send blessings upon the Prophet. O you who believe, invoke blessings on him and salute him with the salutation of peace. (al-Ahzab 33:56)

One may send a short or long blessing upon the Prophet. The few short ones are as follows:

May Allah's blessing and peace be upon him!	صَلَّى اللهُ عَلَيْهِ وَسَلَّمْ
May peace be upon him! (for all Prophets)	عَلَيْهِ السَّلاَمُ
May blessing be upon him!	عَلَيْهِ الصَّلوٰةُ
May Allah's blessing and peace be upon him!	صَلوٰةُ اللهِ عَلَيْهِ وَسَلاَمُهُ

Third, the Islamic courtesy requires that the mention of a name of a Companion of the Prophet should be followed by saying:

May Allah be pleased with him! رَضِيَ اللهُ عَنْهُ

In case of the fourth Caliph, 'Ali ibn Abi Talib, one may say:

May Allah honor his face! كَرَّمَ اللهُ وَجْهَهُ

The readers are requested that they invoke appropriate blessings as mentioned above while reading this book.

TABLE 1: TRANSLITERATION TABLE OF ARABIC ALPHABET

No	Consonants	Name	Transliteration / Pronunciation	
1	ء	hamza	’	as in awful (when strongly emphasized)
2	ا	alif	a	as in all
3	ب	bā	b	as in boy
4	ت	tā	t	soft sound of t as in theatre or as pronounced by an Italian
5	ث	thā	th	as in think
6	ج	jim	j	as in John
7	ح	ḥā	ḥ	no equivalent English sound*
8	خ	khā	kh	no equivalent sound in English* (strong guttural)
9	د	dal	d	as in width
10	ذ	dhal	dh	more emphatic than ‘th’ in that
11	ر	rā	r, r’	thin and thick sound of English r respectively
12	ز	zay	z	as in zoo
13	س	sin	s	as in sound
14	ش	shin	sh	as in shallow
15	ص	ṣād	ṣ	as in saw
16	ض	ḍād	ḍ	no equivalent English sound*
17	ط	ṭā	ṭ	no equivalent English sound*
18	ظ	ẓā	ẓ	no equivalent English sound*
19	ع	‘ain	‘	no equivalent English sound*
20	غ	ghain	gh	a sort of gargling sound as in ghoul
21	ف	fā	f	as in fox
22	ق	qāf	q	no equivalent English sound*
23	ك	kaf	k	as in king
24	ل	lām	I, I	thin and thick sound of English I respectively
25	م	mīm	m	as in moon
26	ن	nūn	n	as in noon, or as in uncle (nasal sound)
27	ه	hā	h	heat as in
28	و	waw	w	as in walk (with ḥaraka) as in fool (when sākin)
29	ي	yā	y	as in yard (beginning sound) as in speed (middle or ending sound)

* See Chapter Three on “Places and Manners of Articulation” for correct pronunciation.

CHART 1 : THE RULES OF TAJWĪD

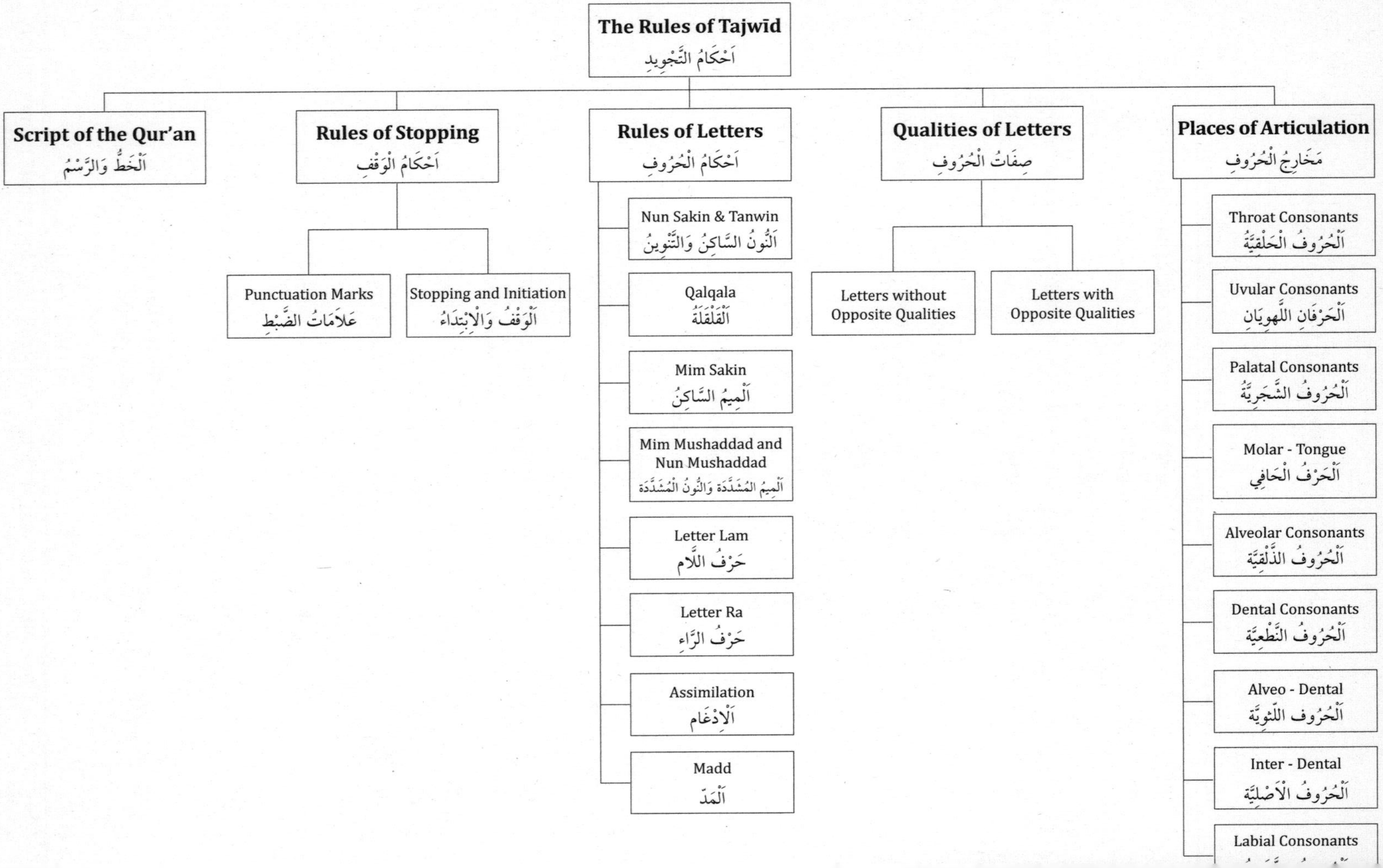
The Rules of Tajwīd
اَحْكَامُ التَّجْوِيدِ
Script of the Qur'an
اَلْخَطُّ وَالرَّسْمُ
Rules of Stopping
اَحْكَامُ الْوَقْفِ
Punctuation Marks
عَلَامَاتُ الضَّبْطِ
Stopping and Initiation
اَلْوَقْفُ وَالْاِبْتِدَاءُ
Rules of Letters
اَحْكَامُ الْحُرُوفِ
Nun Sakin & Tanwin
اَلنُّونُ السَّاكِنُ وَالتَّنْوِينُ
Qalqala
اَلْقَلْقَلَةُ
Mim Sakin
اَلْمِيمُ السَّاكِنُ
Mim Mushaddad and Nun Mushaddad
اَلْمِيمُ الْمُشَدَّدَة وَالنُّونُ الْمُشَدَّدَة
Letter Lam
حَرْفُ اللَّام
Letter Ra
حَرْفُ الرَّاءِ
Assimilation
اَلْاِدْغَام
Madd
اَلْمَدّ
Qualities of Letters
صِفَاتُ الْحُرُوفِ
Letters without Opposite Qualities
Letters with Opposite Qualities
Places of Articulation
مَخَارِجُ الْحُرُوفِ
Throat Consonants
اَلْحُرُوفُ الْحَلْقِيَّةُ
Uvular Consonants
اَلْحَرْفَانِ اللَّهوِيَانِ
Palatal Consonants
اَلْحُرُوفُ الشَّجَرِيَّةُ
Molar - Tongue
اَلْحَرْفُ الْحَافِي
Alveolar Consonants
اَلْحُرُوفُ الذَّلْقِيَّة
Dental Consonants
اَلْحُرُوفُ النَّطْعِيَّة
Alveo - Dental
اَلْحُرُوف اللِّثوِيَّة
Inter - Dental
اَلْحُرُوفُ الْاَصْلِيَّة
Labial Consonants

Chapter One

INTRODUCTION TO TAJWĪD

Introduction to Tajwīd

Arabic is usually classified into three categories:

1. Classical Arabic,
2. Modern literary Arabic,
3. Modern spoken or colloquial Arabic.

Classical Arabic dates from the 6th century (CE). It is the sacred language of the Qur'an. It attained a dominance not only in Arabia but throughout the lands of Islam.

Being the Divine Revelation and the cornerstone of Islam, the recitation of a portion from the Holy Qur'an forms an essential part of the Daily Prayers in public or private. Its perusal is in itself a meritorious act of worship, and its repetition with the intention to memorize and recite it is a great privilege. Of all the Scriptures, the Qur'an alone, definitely and emphatically, is entirely the Word of God in both its language and meaning. It was revealed to the Prophet Muhammad, peace and blessings be upon him, gradually, over approximately twenty-three years (610–632 CE), through the angel of revelation, Jibril (Gabriel) and is in accord with human nature in every way. It is available today in the original form and in a living and progressive Arabic language of great refinement and literature. In fact, the Qur'an is the only Scripture which is read in its original text throughout the world.

The Qur'an is an illumination and a light; it is a guidance for humankind and jinn, delivering the believers from error and deception; and it a healing for spiritual diseases.

﴿وَنُنَزِّلُ مِنَ الْقُرْآنِ مَا هُوَ شِفَاءٌ وَرَحْمَةٌ لِلْمُؤْمِنِينَ
وَلاَ يَزِيدُ الظَّالِمِينَ إِلاَّ خَسَارًا﴾

We send down [stage by stage] in the Qur'an that which is a [spiritual] healing and a mercy to those who believe. (al-Isrā' 17:82)

The Qur'an is the strong rope of Allah which man should grasp firmly. It is the strongest and the most dependable support which man should take hold of. It is the Divine guidance for all humanity to come until the Last Day. It is a clear light in which a man should walk in his life. One who has believed in it, has indeed been blessed and favored by Allah; one who has professed its tenets and principles, has surely spoken the truth; one who has held fast to it, has really become rightly guided; one who has acted in accordance with it, has certainly achieved success. The reading or recitation of the Qur'an is enjoined by Allah the Almighty and His Messenger upon every believer, man and woman, young and old alike. Islam teaches that the love of Allah and His Messenger is the loftiest ideal for man:

﴿قُلْ إِنْ كَانَ اٰبَاؤُكُمْ وَأَبْنَاؤُكُمْ وَإِخْوَانُكُمْ وَأَزْوَاجُكُمْ وَعَشِيرَتُكُمْ وَأَمْوَالٌ اقْتَرَفْتُمُوهَا
وَتِجَارَةٌ تَخْشَوْنَ كَسَادَهَا وَمَسَاكِنُ تَرْضَوْنَهَا أَحَبَّ إِلَيْكُمْ مِنَ اللّٰهِ وَرَسُولِهِ وَجِهَادٍ فِي
سَبِيلِهِ فَتَرَبَّصُوا حَتَّى يَأْتِيَ اللّٰهُ بِأَمْرِهِ وَاللّٰهُ لَا يَهْدِي الْقَوْمَ الْفَاسِقِينَ﴾

> Say: "If it be that your fathers, your children, your brothers, your mates, or your kindred, the wealth that ye have gained the commerce in which ye fear a decline, or the dwellings in which ye delight, are dearer to you than God, or His Messenger, or the striving in His cause, then wait until God brings about His decree. God guides not the rebellious." (at-Tawbah 9:24)

One who loves God and the Prophet will naturally have the love for the Qur'an as well. Its Divine words are transmitted, for the benefit of humankind, through Prophet Muhammad, peace and blessings be upon him.

The words of the Qur'an must not be read hastily merely to increase the score of reading. They themselves are so beautiful that they must be lovingly pronounced in tones of rhythmic expression. According to a tradition, the Noble Prophet said, "Whosoever recites a single letter of the Book of Allah will have a good deed credited to him, and the reward of any good deed will be multiplied by ten." (at-Tirmidhi, Jami', II, 150).

Thus, a man who reads only the translation of the Qur'an will be deprived of the blessing and benediction[1] which emanate from reciting the Qur'an itself. The proper recitation of the Qur'an can be achieved by following the methods appropriate to Divine Speech. Since the Qur'an is the Divine Speech, both in words and in meaning, and whose recitation is an act of worship, the methodology of reading or studying an ordinary book taught in today's western style schools is not relevant and applicable to the recitation of the Holy Qur'an. It must be intoned, not just read or recited as one might read an ordinary document. The Almighty Allah Himself has said:

---

1 Benediction: a short blessing with which public worship is concluded.

﴿وَرَتِّلِ الْقُرْآنَ تَرْتِيلاً﴾

And recite the Qur'an in slow, measured rhythmic tones. (al-Muzzammil 73:4)

The word "rattil" (رَتِّل) in the verse under discussion means "to recite in slow, measured rhythmic tones" or "to recite with calm and distinct enunciation, gracefully and with intonation." It also means "to set in order," and when used in speech it means "to speak orderly and correctly."[2] As a consequence, there developed the art of *Tajwīd*—a method of Qur'anic recitation. The word "tajwīd" (اَلتَّجْوِيد) is the verbal noun of the verb "jawwada" (جَوَّدَ) which means "to make things excellent." A statement ascribed to the Prophet's close Companion Abdullah ibn Mas'ud reads: "Jawwidu'l-Qur'an"—recite the Qur'an well.[3] It is reported that he devoted much effort to developing Tartīl (تَرْتِيل) and Tajwīd (اَلتَّجْوِيد) in the recitation of the Qur'an. Canonical Hadith collections of al-Bukhari and Muslim report the tradition of how the Holy Prophet used to weep when Ibn Mas'ud recited the Qur'an and instructed his followers to imitate the way Ibn Mas'ud recited.[4] Ibn Mas'ud is reported to have said that the Qur'anic recitation be "neither as prosaic as the dispersing of dates nor as recitative as the rendering of poetry."[5] In the lifetime of the Holy Prophet there was a distinctive style of utterance; a kind of cantillation producing effects pleasing to the listeners. It delighted the ear, moved the heart and captured the mind.[6] Tradition says that it was the concern for corruptions creeping in that had led 'Uthman, the third Caliph, to issue his canonical standard text,[7] that led Hajjaj ibn Yousuf, in spite of the opposition of many of the old believers, to have the diacritical marks, vocalization and orthographic[8] signs added to the 'Uthmanic text of the Holy Qur'an.[9] But it was the preoccupation of so many pious Muslims with the correct reading and proper interpretation of their Scripture which quickened interest in all forms of grammatical and linguistic study.[10] It was Ibn Mas'ud who told the Muslims: "Adore the Qur'anic recitation and ornament it by the finest intonation."[11] The attempt to do this produced Tajwīd. The details of this art of recitation are presented in the following chapters of this book.

---

2 Tabari, *Tafsir*, XXIX, 80, gives this original meaning.

3 Suyuti, *al-Itqan fi 'Ulum al-Qur'an* (The Perfect Guide to the Sciences of the Qur'an), I, 102.

4 See Abu Hanifa, Musnad, p. 37; quoted in K. I. Semaan, p. 32.

5 Ibn al-Jazari, *Kitab al-Nashr*, I, p. 207, Damascus, 1345 AH.
لاَ تَنْثُرُوهُ يَعْنِى الْقُرْآنَ نَثْرَ الدَّقْلِ وَلاَ تَهذُوهُ هَذيَ الشِّعْرِ.

6 Ibn al-Jazari, *Kitab al-Nashr*, I, p. 212.

7 Al-Bukhari, Sahih, III, 393; al-Tabari: Tafsir I, 21; Abu Dawud: Masahif, pp. 18-19.

8 The representation of the sounds of a language by written symbols.

9 Supra, p. 19.

10 K. I. Semaan, *Linguistics in the Middle Ages*, Leiden, Netherlands, 1968.

11 جَوِّدُوا الْقُرْآنَ وَزَيِّنُوهُ بِأَحْسَنِ الْأَصْوَاتِ

What Is Tajwīd?

The Arabic equivalents for "reading" are *Qirā'a* and *Tilāwa*. Both terms have now been used in connection with the reading of the Qur'an. In the beginning, however, the word "Qirā'a" was used particularly for learning the Qur'an and acquiring its knowledge, and a "Qārī" (قَارِئٌ) was originally a scholar of the Qur'an. As time passed, the term was gradually drifted from its original meaning and torn into two parts:

(1) The word "Qirā'a" began to be used for reading the Qur'an with correct pronunciation and modulation according to the rules of Tajwīd,

(2) The word "Tilāwa" came to be used as a general term for reading the Holy Book with fervor and devotion for the purpose of seeking guidance and blessings.

The rules of the correct recitation of the Qur'an are to be taken from the Qur'an, the Traditions of the Prophet, and faithful Companions of the Prophet.

The Holy Qur'an briefly mentions some of the befitting methods relevant to proper and attentive recitation:

﴿وَرَتِّلِ الْقُرْآنَ تَرْتِيلاً﴾

And recite the Qur'an in slow, measured rhythmic tones. (al-Muzzammil 73:4)

﴿فَإِذَا قَرَأْتَ الْقُرْآنَ فَاسْتَعِذْ بِاللهِ مِنَ الشَّيْطَانِ الرَّجِيمِ﴾

When you read the Qur'an, seek God's protection from Satan, the rejected one. (an-Nahl 16:98)

﴿أَفَلاَ يَتَدَبَّرُونَ الْقُرْآنَ أَمْ عَلَى قُلُوبٍ أَقْفَالُهَا﴾

Do they not then earnestly seek to understand the Qur'an, or are there locks on their hearts? (Muhammad 47:24)

﴿إِنَّمَا الْمُؤْمِنُونَ الَّذِينَ إِذَا ذُكِرَ اللهُ وَجِلَتْ قُلُوبُهُمْ وَإِذَا تُلِيَتْ عَلَيْهِمْ ءَايَاتُهُ زَادَتْهُمْ إِيمَانًا وَعَلَى رَبِّهِمْ يَتَوَكَّلُونَ﴾

For, believers are those who, when God is mentioned, feel a tremor in their hearts, and when they hear His Signs rehearsed, find their faith strengthened, and put [all] their trust in their Lord. (al-Anfal 8:2)

﴿إِذَا تُتْلَى عَلَيْهِمْ ءَايَاتُ الرَّحْمٰنِ خَرُّوا سُجَّدًا وَبُكِيًّا﴾

Whenever the Signs of [God] the Most Gracious, were rehearsed to them, they would fall down in prostrate adoration and tears. (Maryam 19:58)

We find from the study of the Qur'an itself that the Holy Prophet, in the earliest days of his Messengership, was specially instructed to stand for the greater part of the night to Prayers before his Lord, reciting the Qur'an in slow, rhythmic tones:

﴿يَا أَيُّهَا الْمُزَّمِّلُ ۝ قُمِ اللَّيْلَ إِلاَّ قَلِيلاً ۝ نِصْفَهُ أَوِ انْقُصْ مِنْهُ قَلِيلاً ۝ أَوْ زِدْ عَلَيْهِ وَرَتِّلِ الْقُرْآنَ تَرْتِيلاً﴾

O thou folded in garment! Stand [to Prayers] by night, but not all night—half of it—or a little less, or a little more; and recite the Qur'an in slow, measured rhythmic tones. (al-Muzzammil 73:1–4)

﴿وَ أُمِرْتُ أَنْ أَكُونَ مِنَ الْمُسْلِمِينَ ۝ وَأَنْ أَتْلُوَ الْقُرْآنَ ﴾

And I am commanded [by God] to be one of the Muslims, and to recite the Qur'an. (an-Naml 27:91–92)

In the later stages of his Messengership, the special instruction he received from his Lord was to recite the Qur'an:

﴿وَاتْلُ مَا أُوحِيَ إِلَيْكَ مِنْ كِتَابِ رَبِّكَ لاَ مُبَدِّلَ لِكَلِمَاتِهِ وَلَنْ تَجِدَ مِنْ دُونِهِ مُلْتَحَدًا﴾

And recite what has been revealed to thee of the Book of thy Lord: none can change His Words, and none wilt thou find as a refuge other than Him. (al-Kahf 18:27)

Again, a similar instruction was repeated in the following verse:

﴿اتْلُ مَا أُوحِيَ إِلَيْكَ مِنَ الْكِتَابِ وَأَقِمِ الصَّلَاةَ﴾

And recite what is sent of the Book by inspiration to thee, and establish regular Prayers. (al-Ankabut 29:45)

The following verse from the Sūra al-Baqara describes how the receivers of the Qur'an manifested their great regards for this Book:

﴿الَّذِينَ آتَيْنَاهُمُ الْكِتَابَ يَتْلُونَهُ حَقَّ تِلَاوَتِهِ أُولَٰئِكَ يُؤْمِنُونَ بِهِ﴾

Those to whom We have delivered the Book, recite it as it ought to be recited; they believe in it. (al-Baqara 2:121)

The recitation of the Qur'an in its real sense is an activity in which the tongue, the intellect, and the mind all take part. The part which the tongue plays consists in the correct pronunciation of letters in a slow and distinct manner. The part played by the intellect lies in explaining the meaning. The part which the mind plays is to accept warnings given and to feel as a result of being checked against the forbidden things and obeying the commandments.[12]

A vast majority of the Muslim youths, even a large number of adults and old people among us, cannot recite the Qur'an. This lack of ability to read even the bare text of the Qur'an is due to two reasons:

1- The decline of classical system of education that was imparted in the Masjid and the Madrasa to all the children of the community,

2- The popularity of the kindergarten and other types of modern primary schools which do not include the recitation of the Qur'an in their curriculum.

Those who do not possess the ability to properly read the Qur'an should realize their deficiency and take necessary steps to improve it. All Islamic centers and schools throughout the world should adopt it as a decided policy that the education of their children will start with Tajwīd and the first thing they will learn will be how to say the Divine Words of everyday use properly.

It is incumbent on every Muslim to acquire the competence of reciting the Qur'an with a correct accent and pronunciation, carefully observing all the rules of the Tajwīd. It is also required for the correct recitation of the Qur'an that it be read in the best manner and in the most melodious voice. Every human being is gifted

---

[12] Al-Ghazali, *al-Ihya al-'Ulumu'd-Din* (The Revival of the Religious Sciences).

with a love for music and has a natural fondness for sweet and melodious sounds. Islam, being a natural religion, does not curb any of the inherent tendencies but channelizes them into healthy and ethical forms.

The Noble Prophet told his followers about the rewards of reciting, studying and teaching the Qur'an as follows:

> Recite the Qur'an, for it will come on the Day of Resurrection to intercede for its companion. (Sahih Muslim, Musafirin, 252)

خَيْرُكُمْ مَنْ تَعَلَّمَ الْقُرْآنَ وَعَلَّمَهُ

> The best among you are those who learn the Qur'an and teach it to others. (al-Bukhari, Sahih, Fada'il al-Qur'an, Ibn Maja, Muqaddama, 16; ad-Darimi, Fada'il al-Qur'an, 2)

> Allah says: "The one who recites the Qur'an, and is thereby prevented from supplicating to Me and making petition to Me, is indeed given by Me the best of the reward of those who are grateful to Me." (at-Tirmidhi, Thawab al-Qur'an, 25, ad-Darimi, Fada'il al-Qur'an, 6)

> Those who are concerned with the Qur'an are friends of Allah and are special to Him. (Ibn Hanbal, III, 128, 242)

Here "those who are concerned with the Qur'an" refers to those believers who safeguard it and adhere firmly to it by reciting and memorizing it and by acting upon its teachings.

To fulfill this important obligation, one must learn how the Qur'an ought to be recited and what steps should be taken if the required standard of recitation is to be attained. In this connection, the first step is to acquire a thorough knowledge of the Arabic alphabet, their correct phonetic articulation, the qualities of certain letters with which they are pronounced and the significance of different kinds of punctuation marks used in the Qur'an. The technical term used for this knowledge is Tajwīd which is a must for a good, correct, and fluent recitation of the Qur'an.

As everyone has instinctive love for the beauty of the sight and the beauty of the sound, one should insist upon a fascinating printing of the Holy Qur'an and its recitation in a soft melodious voice. The Holy Prophet has urged us as follows:

زَيِّنُوا الْقُرْآنَ بِأَصْوَاتِكُمْ

> Adorn the Qur'an with your voice. (al-Bukhari, Sahih, Tawhid, 52; Abu Dawud, Sunan, Witr, 20; an-Nasai, Sunan, Iftitah, 83; Ibn Maja, Sunan, Iqama, 176)

He is also quoted as saying:

مَا اَذَنَ اللّٰهُ لِشَيءٍ مَا اَذَنَهُ لِحُسْنِ الصَّوْتِ بِالْقُرْآنِ

Allah does not listen to anything so attentively as He listens to the Qur'an being recited in a sweet voice. (al-Bukhari, Sahih, Tawhid, 32, 52, Fada'il al-Qur'an, 19; Muslim, Sahih, Musafirin, 232, 233, 234.)

It is stated in the traditions and sayings of the Holy Prophet that once he heard Abu Musa recite the Qur'an in a melodious voice, he praised him in these words:

This man is bestowed with the sweet voice of [Prophet] Dawud. (al-Bukhari, Sahih, Fada'il al-Qur'an, 31; Muslim, Sahih, Musafirin, 235, 23.)

Although a person should recite the Qur'an in the most melodious voice, yet to over-emphasize this aspect of recitation is not without danger. When the melodious recitation is the outcome of *riyā'*—mere show or ostentation,[13] or singing, it becomes a serious perversion and a reprehensible practice.

[13] It is defined as the desire to please men through a devotional act and is strongly prohibited in the Qur'an (See 2:264, 4:38, 4:142, 8:47, 107:6).

The Need for Tajwīd

The difference between classical and colloquial Arabic may be analyzed under three headings: phonology,[14] grammar, and vocabulary. Our concern in Tajwīd lies in phonology. A comprehensive study in the phonology of the main dialect area of the Arabic speaking countries is well beyond the scope of this book. The following notes are intended only to show non-Arabic speaking people why it is important to understand, practice, and master the art of Tajwīd. The Arabic speaking Muslims should also practice and acquire the art of Tajwīd because in most of the Arabic dialects the pronunciation of certain letters of the Arabic differs to some extent from that of the recognized classical usage. Generally speaking, consonants difficult to pronounce are simplified. This simplification, while permitted in colloquial usage, is in contradiction with the rules of Tajwīd. The following brief account gives the variation of the Arabic alphabet in Arabic speaking countries.

1. The hamza (ء) goes frequently unpronounced except at the beginning of a word. For example:

قَرَأَ *qara'* is pronounced as *qarā* قَرَا

رِيَاءً *riyā'* is pronounced as *riyā* رِيَا

لُؤْلُؤ *lu'lu'* is pronounced as *lu lu* لُولُو

2. The consonant ث (thā) becomes either tā (ت) or sīn (س). For example:

ثَلَاثَةٌ (thalātha) is pronounced as talāta (تَلَاتَةٌ)

مَثَلًا (mathalan) is pronounced as masalan (مَسَلًا) or matalan (مَتَلًا) as is usually heard in some parts of Syria and Lebanon.

3. The consonant ج (jim) becomes hard "g" (گ) in Egyptian Arabic. For example:

مَجِيدٌ *Majīd* is pronounced as *Magīd* مَگِيدٌ

جَمَال *Jamāl* is pronounced as *Gamāl* گَمَال

4. The consonant ذ (dhal) is substituted by د (dal) or ز (zay). For example:

هٰذَا *hadha* is pronounced as *hada* هٰدَا

كَذٰلِكَ *kadhālik* is pronounced as *kazālik* كَزٰلِك

Note: Iraq and the Arabian peninsula are exception.

---

[14] Phonology is the science of speech sounds in a language.

5. The letter ض (ḍād) is usually considered a peculiar Arabic sound, yet it is frequently confused with ظ (ẓā). In Iraq and areas in the Arabian peninsula, both these letters have a sound similar to that of ذ (dhal). In Egypt and the Levant the letter ظ (ẓā) is sometimes pronounced as ض (ḍād) in addition to its own sound as ظ (ẓā). For example:

ضَابِطٌ ḍābit is pronounced as zābit زَابِطٌ in Egypt and the Levant.

مَضْبُوطٌ maḍbūt is pronounced both as maẓbūt مَظْبُوطٌ and maḍbūt مَضْبُوطٌ in Syria and Lebanon.

6. The other alphabet have the following variations in different regions:

– In lower Egypt, Syria, Lebanon, occupied Palestine and western areas of Jordan, ق (qāf) becomes (ء) hamza. For example:

قَالَ qāla is pronounced as 'ala اَلْ

– In Sudan, parts of Iraq, the Arabian peninsula, Tunisia, Algeria, and Morocco ق (qāf) is pronounced as hard "g" as in the English word "good." For example:

قَالَ qāla is pronounced as gāla كَالَ

7. Considerable divergence is found in the vowel sounds in the colloquial from the classical Arabic. For example:

ضَمَّةٌ (ḍamma) often becomes كَسْرَةٌ (kasra)

حُسَيْنٌ Husain may be heard as حَسَيْنٌ Hisain

فَتْحَةٌ Fatha is often not sounded at all or distinctively

كَبِيرٌ Kabīr is pronounced as كِبِيرٌ Kibīr

Diphthongs may become vowels and vice versa.

Khalil I. Semaan[15] has presented several stories related to Arabic grammatical interest and linguistics. From the point of view of Tajwīd , a couple of them are presented below to show how mispronunciation of a single letter can change the entire meaning:

1. Ziyad ibn Abih,[16] the governor of the two Iraqs, was bothered by the way the new Muslims in that area made grave mistakes in reading the Qur'an. He begged Abu al-Aswad to make available the grammatical knowledge he had learned from the Prophet's son-in-law, 'Ali ibn Abi Talib', in order to help the Muslims to understand the Qur'an better.

Abu al-Aswad was unwilling to do this until one day he himself heard a man recite the third verse of Sūra at-Tawbah, reading وَرَسُولِهِ (wa rasūlihi) when he should have read وَرَسُولُهُ (wa rasūluhu) and so making the passage mean:

God is free from obligation to the idolaters and His Messenger.

---

[15]   Khalil I. Semaan, *Linguistics in the Middle Ages*, Leiden, Netherlands, 1968.

[16]   The earliest form of the narration goes back to the Prophet's Companion Abu 'Ubaida (d. 210 AH/825 CE) from whom it is quoted by al-Sirafi, *Akhbar*, p. 15.

instead of

﴿أَنَّ اللهَ بَرِيءٌ مِّنَ الْمُشْرِكِينَ وَرَسُولُهُ...﴾

God is free from obligation to the idolaters, and (so is) His Messenger. (at-Tawbah 9:3)

Abu al-Aswad was so horrified by this mispronunciation of the Divine Message that he went back to the governor and asked him that a good scribe be brought and large codex of the Qur'an be produced, whereat, he asked the scribe to put marks to indicate the *fatha, kasra,* and *ḍamma* on each word, so that there could be no more confusion in reading.

2. Another narration[17] recounts how a convert to Islam, who had taken the Arabic name Sa'd (سَعْدٌ), came to Abu al-Aswad in Basra, seeking his help to approach Qudamah ibn Maz'un[18] with whom he was anxious to enter into client relationship. As he was leading his horse and not riding it, Abu al-Aswad asked him "What is the matter O Sa'd? Why are you not riding?" However, he pronounced the word for limping as "*dali*" (acting wrongfully) instead of "*zali*" (limping). Some of those standing around laughed at him, Abu al-Aswad said, "These are now our Muslim brothers. Would not it be better if instead of laughing at them we tried to teach them to speak Arabic more correctly."

The rules of Tajwīd are necessary in order to convey the correct meaning by uttering the sound of each letter from its proper place and manner of articulation. The most common and frequent errors are those of substitution of *fatha, kasra,* and *ḍamma* and the substitution of one letter by another letter.

The following letters, foreign to English, are most commonly interchanged with their English counterparts and other letters of the Arabic alphabet.

Alphabet foreign to English		**Most frequently substituted by**			
Ṣād	ص	Sīn	س		
Thā	ث	Sīn	س	or Tā	ت
'Ain	ع	Alif	ا	or Hamza	ء
Ḥā	ح	Hā	ه		
Ẓā	ظ	Zay	ز		
Dhāl	ذ	Zay	ز		
Ṭā	ط	Tā	ت		
Ḍād	ض	Dal	د		

17 Al-Sirafi, *Akhbar*, p. 18.

18 A Companion of the Prophet whom 'Umar (the second Caliph) had appointed as governor of the Bahrain area.

A few examples of such mistakes of interchanging of the letters in pronunciation and their corresponding meanings are given below for illustration.

Correctly pronounced		Mispronounced (Substitution of letters)	
أَلْحَمْدُ لِلّٰه	Praise be to God	Starved to death for God	اَلْهَمْدُ لِلّٰه
أَنْعَمْتَ عَلَيْهِمْ	On whom Thou hast bestowed Thy Grace	On whom Thou hast bestowed Thy sleep	اَنَمْتَ عَلَيهِمْ
رَحْمٰنٌ	All-Merciful	Rain cloud	رَهْمَنٌ
ضَآلِّينَ	Astray	Guiders	دَآلِّينَ
ضَلَّ	To error wander	Guide; show	دَلَّ
صَمَدٌ	Eternal; absolute	Hole in the ground with rain water	تَمَدٌ
عَظِيمٌ	Great; excellent	Miserable	اَزِيمٌ
عَلِيمٌ	Full of knowledge	Grievous	اَلِيمٌ
نَصْرٌ	Help	Eagle; vulture; prose	نَسْرٌ، نَثْرٌ
نَسَرَ	To remove; to tear with the beak	To scatter; disperse; to sprinkle	نَثَرَ
عَصْرٌ	Time; age	Difficulty	عَسْرٌ
صَوْمٌ	Fasting	Garlic	ثَوْمٌ
ثَمَّ	There	Poison	سَمَّ
حَرَامٌ	Unlawful in religion; sacred	Pyramid	هَرَامٌ
مَرِيضٌ	Sick; ill	Obstinate in rebellion	مَرِيدٌ
نَبَطَ	To gush out	To germinate; to produce	نَبَتَ
نَصَبٌ	Labor; fatigue	Cosanguinity, (having the same lineage; akin)	نَسَبٌ
نَقْبٌ	To dig through (a wall)	To turn aside	نَكْبٌ
قَلْبٌ	A heart	A dog	كَلْبٌ
حُرٌّ	Free; freeman	A cat	هِرٌّ

Other mistakes due to substitution of *ḍamma*, *fatha*, and *kasra*[19] are as follows:

Word with correct vowel		Word when vowel changed	
حُرٌّ	Free; freeman	Heat	حَرٌّ
جِنَّةٌ	Jinn (genii, demon)	Garden, paradise	جَنَّةٌ
جَمَالٌ	Beauty	Camels	جِمَالٌ
مِنْ	A preposition signifying origin, e.g. from	An indeclinable conjunctive pronoun meaning he, she, or they who, one who, some who, etc.	مَنْ
ثُمَّ	Then	There	ثَمَّ
شِفَاءٌ	Healing	Death	شَفَاءٌ

19 See Chapter Two for detailed explanation of the vowel marks of *ḍamma* (ُ), *fatha* (َ), *kasra* (ِ).

Chapter Two

REVIEW OF ARABIC

THE ARABIC ALPHABET

The Arabic alphabet consists of twenty nine[20] letters which all represent consonants.[21] Since Arabic does not have vowels as letters, indication of vowels is by means of a system of strokes written over or below the consonantal letters. The strokes or diacritics that are called *ḥaraka* (اَلْحَرَكَة) are not usually written except in the Holy Qur'an to ensure exact rendition and to facilitate correct reading.

CONSONANTS

The letter "أ" (*alif*) has no sound of its own but it is used merely as a support for "ء" (*hamza*) under certain conditions or to lengthen a preceding vowel (*madd*) or at the end of third person plural of verbs. The first real consonant, therefore, of the Arabic alphabet is "ء" (*hamza*).[22]

When the letter "ت" (*tā*) is used as the feminine ending of nouns or adjectives, it is written as "ة" (*hā*) with two dots over it and is called "تَاءٌ مَرْبُوطَةٌ" (*tā marbūṭa*).[23] The ordinary "ت" (*tā*) is called "تَاءٌ طَوِيلَةٌ" (*tā ṭawīla*).

"VACANT" (REDUNDANT) LETTERS

Sometimes "ا" (*alif*), "و" (*waw*), and "ي" (*ya*) are written but not pronounced. The conditions under which these letters are written but not pronounced are as follows:

1. LETTER ALIF ("ا"): "ا" (*alif*) is always *sākin* (having no vowel or *ḥaraka*) in Arabic as mentioned earlier. If there is a vowel sign (*ḥaraka*) on it, it is called "ء" (*hamza*). *Alif* ("ا") is always preceded by a letter with *fatha*. This lengthens the pronunciation of *fatha* to two times.

For example:

Mā مَا (where ā = aa)

Lā لَا

---

[20] If "ء" (*hamza*) and "ا" (*alif*) are counted separately.

[21] *Alif, waw,* and *yā* are also used to indicate the long vowel sound. Short vowels are indicated by a system of symbols called *ḍamma, fatha* and *kasra* (ُ , َ , ِ), as explained later in this chapter.

[22] In the copies of the Qur'an printed in the Arab countries, an "ا" (*alif*) is always given the vowel sign (*ḥaraka*) with hamza: أ , إ , أ whereas the copies of the Qur'an printed in Turkey, India, Pakistan, and Bangladesh, "ا" (*alif*) is given the *ḥaraka* with fatha, ḍamma, or kasra: اَ , اِ , اُ

[23] It is also called "تَاءٌ مُدَوَّرَة" (Round Tā "ة") or "تَاءٌ تَأْنِيث" (Tā of feminine ending "ـة").

Alif is completely ignored in the following cases:

(a) If it is followed by a letter with *sukūn* (absence of *ḥaraka*) or *tashdīd* (shadda) sign over it. For Example:

Pronounced as	Written as
مَلْكِتَابُ وَلَلْاِيمَانُ	مَا الْكِتَابُ وَلَا الْاِيمَانُ
مَلّٰه مُبْدِيه	مَا اللّٰه مُبْدِيه
لَسَّيِّئَةُ	لَا السَّيِّئَةُ

(b) In the first person singular اَنَا, if followed by a *sākin* or *mushaddad* letter, the alif is ignored and no small circle is placed over it in all such cases. For example:

اَنَا اخْتَرْتُكَ فَاسْتَمِعْ لِمَا يُوحَى

اِنَّنِي اَنَا اللّٰهُ

(c) An alif is written but not pronounced after the *sākin* "و" (waw). For example:

كَتَبُوا = كَتَبُو

كَانُوا = كَانُو

(d) An alif is not pronounced if followed by a *sākin* letter. For example:

فَادْعُ = فَدْعُ

(e) An alif is ignored if preceded by a letter with *kasra*. For example:

مِائَةَ = مِئَةَ

2. LETTER WAW (و): The letter waw will be written but not pronounced if there is no vowel (*ḥaraka*) on it, i.e. it is *sākin*. For example:

صَلٰوتُكَ = صَلٰتُكَ

3. LETTER YĀ (ي): The letter yā will be ignored in pronunciation if it is written without a vowel (*ḥaraka*) on it or without dots under it. For example:

FIL KITĀBI	فِى الْكِتَابِ = فِلْكِتَابِ	no *ḥaraka* on yā
BALĀ	بَلَى = بَلَا	no dots under yā

THE ARABIC VOWELS

Indication of the vowel sounds in Arabic are by means of a system of strokes adjacent to the consonantal characters. Every consonant in Arabic is provided with a vowel sound (*ḥaraka*) or with a sign indicating its absence (*sukūn*).

THE VOWELS

1. FATHA (فَتْحَةٌ) is a small diagonal stroke over a consonant ـَ . For example:

صَدَقَ / نَقَبَ / نَبَطَ

2. KASRA (كَسْرَةٌ) is a small diagonal stroke under a consonant ـِ . For example:

مِنْ / فِي / عِلْمٌ

3. ḌAMMA (ضَمَّةٌ) is a small waw over a consonant ـُ . For example:

يُوسُفُ / قُرْآنٌ / قُلْ

SUKŪN (اَلسُّكُونُ):

The sign indicating the absence of a vowel is written directly above a consonant. It is called a *sukūn* (اَلسُّكُون) or a *jazma* (اَلْجَزْمَةُ), or al-jazm. For example: كُنْ

In addition to three vowel signs indicated above, long vowels and diphthongs are also possible when vowel is followed by a madd letter (alif, waw, or yā).

1. Short vowels		Transliteration	Vowel sound	Example	
Fatha	ـَ	a	as in polar	Lan	لَنْ
Kasra	ـِ	i	as in sin	Jinn	جِنْ
Ḍamma	ـُ	u	as in put	Kun	كُنْ

2. Long Vowels	Transliteration	Vowel sound	Example	
ـَ + ا	ā	as in father	Lā	لَا
ـِ + ي	ī	as in me	Lī	لِي
ـُ + و	ū	as in rule	Nūr	نُورٌ

3. Diphthongs[24]

ـَ + ي	ai	as in paid	Saifun	سَيْفٌ
ـَ + و	au	as in taught	Khaufun	خَوْفٌ

24 When Waw Sākin and Yā Sākin are preceded by *fatha*, they are known as Līn letters and pronounced softly. See "Qualities of the Letters" in Chapter Four.

THE TASHDĪD OR SHADDA

When a consonant occurs twice without a vowel sound in between, it is written once only and the sign (ّ) is placed over it. This (ّ) sign is called *tashdīd* (تَشْدِيدٌ) or *shadda* (شَدَّةٌ) and the letter is called *mushaddad* (مُشَدَّدٌ). The *mushaddad* letter is pronounced twice, the first one always *sākin* and the second one with a vowel sound (fatha, kasra, or ḍamma).

The *shadda* can occur due to complete merger of lām of definite article[25] as in *ash-shams* اَلشَّمْسُ or it may be part of the word form as in:

Kasara كَسَرَ (he broke) (no *shadda* on sīn س) but *kassara* كَسَّرَ (he smashed) (with *shadda* on sīn س).

EXAMPLES:

PRONOUNCED		WRITTEN
مَرْرَ	=	مَرَّ
مَارْرُنْ	=	مَارٌّ
تَنَفْفَسَ	=	تَنَفَّسَ
حَبْبَ	=	حَبَّ
ثُوْوِبَ	=	ثُوِّبَ
اَذْذِنْ	=	اَذِّنْ

[25] The detailed discussion on *Idghām* (Merger) will be found in Chapter Four.

TANWĪN (NUNATION)

Tanwīn means to pronounce the sound of the letter "ن" (nūn). At the end of nouns and adjectives, "نُونْ سَاكِنْ" (*nūn sākin*) is not written but it is pronounced. This is called tanwīn or nunation and expressed with double fatha (ـً), double kasra (ـٍ), double ḍamma (ـٌ) and pronounced as AN, IN and UN respectively.

1. DOUBLE FATHA (ـً) (فَتْحَتَيْن) is pronounced by taking only one fatha ـَ and combining it with "نُونْ سَاكِنْ" (*nūn sākin*). For example:

	PRONOUNCED		WRITTEN
TIJĀRATAN	تِجَارَتَنْ	=	تِجَارَةً
NISĀ'AN	نِسَآءَنْ	=	نِسَآءً
RAHMATAN	رَحْمَتَنْ	=	رَحْمَةً

When the sign of double fatha occurs on alif, this alif is ignored and the sound of preceding letter is used with *nūn sākin*. For example:

	PRONOUNCED		WRITTEN
JANAFAN	جَنَفَنْ	=	جَنَفًا

2. DOUBLE KASRA (ـٍ) (كَسْرَتَيْن) is pronounced by taking only one kasra ـِ and combining it with *nūn sākin*. For example:

	PRONOUNCED		WRITTEN
SIYĀMIN	صِيَامِنْ	=	صِيَامٍ
MADADIN	مَدَدِنْ	=	مَدَدٍ
MALAKIN	مَلَكِنْ	=	مَلَكٍ

3. DOUBLE ḌAMMA (ـٌ) (ضَمَّتَيْن) is pronounced by taking only one ḍamma ـُ and combining it with *nūn sākin*. For example:

	PRONOUNCED		WRITTEN
FALAKUN	فَلَكُنْ	=	فَلَكٌ
KHAUFUN	خَوْفُنْ	=	خَوْفٌ
KITĀBUN	كِتَابُنْ	=	كِتَابٌ

GHUNNA (NASALIZATION)

The word "غُنَّة" (*ghunna*) in Arabic means chanting of birds usually heard in the early morning or just before sunset. The Arabs call it غَنَّ الطَّائِرُ.[26] In tajwīd, it is a nasal sound articulated from the nasal cavity known as *khayshum* (اَلْخَيْشُومُ). There are two letters ("ن" *nūn* and "م" *mīm*) that can be pronounced from the nasal cavity by passing the air through the nose. The nasalization or *ghunna* is a quality which depends on certain conditions which will be covered in detail under the title of "The Qualities of the Alphabet" in Chapter Four.

The point of articulation of nasal nūn and mīm for partial or complete *ghunna* is explained in Chapter Three, Phonetics. The nasal sound can be heard in the pronounciation of the English word 'uncle'. The nasal sound can also be easily noticed in certain French words such as Bien (well), Mon (my), Monsieur (Mr.), etc. The nasal sound gives Arabic language distinct characteristics which are not found in English and many other languages.

---

[26] غَنَّ الطَّائِرُ means "The birds sang."

CHAPTER THREE

PHONETICS

PHONETIC DESCRIPTION

Phonetics is the systematic study of speech sound. This study involves:

1. The production of the sound, physiologically and acoustically
2. The transmission of the sound by the air
3. The perception of the sounds, which may be subdivided into their reception and their interpretation.

In this chapter those aspects which lend themselves most readily to objective analysis of the Arabic letters will be dealt with most fully. Any written or printed discussion of phonetics would be greatly handicapped without a relatively simple set of symbols to indicate the sound being discussed. The principle requirement of a phonetic symbol is that there should be but one symbol for each sound, and that no sound shall be represented by more than one symbol. It is also very desirable that the transliteration symbols used should be as familiar to the reader as possible. Arbitrary symbols such as ð, Θ, ʒ, ǣ and ə are difficult to learn and therefore should be avoided.

The Latin alphabet, used for the conventional spelling of English, contain only twenty six letters. There are, however, twenty nine sounds in Arabic. It is, therefore, impossible to represent all Arabic sounds unambiguously by means of the ordinary Latin alphabet. Furthermore, there is no one-to-one correspondence between the Latin and the Arabic alphabet. Therefore, new symbols are introduced in order to represent additional sounds in Arabic, as shown in the Transliteration Table 1.

In structure, Arabic is radically different from English and other well-known languages. Its sound system includes six throat consonants (ه , خ , غ , ح , ع and ء) of particular difficulty for a speaker of English and there are a series of emphatic consonants (ص , ض , ط and ظ) which influence strongly the pronunciation of surrounding vowels. The presence of these consonants, alteration of consonants and vowels, and the emphatic features of pronunciation give the Arabic language a unique characteristic sound which sets it apart from other languages.

TRANSLITERATION

There are quite a variety of symbols currently in use to represent the non-English sounds of Arabic emphatic and throat consonants. As mentioned in the previous section, this is very confusing to the reader when the Arabic words are transliterated into English. Most common representation of these peculiar sounds that are absent in the English are by such symbols as ð, Θ, ʒ, æ, ə, etc. These symbols do not form any logical basis and are very confusing as well as difficult to remember.

The transliteration system presented here is derived after a careful and thoughtful study of the phonetics of Arabic consonants and only those symbols are used which form some logical scheme.

1. The letters س (sīn), د (dāl), ت (tā) and ز (zay) are usually represented by the English letters s, d, t, and z respectively. Whereas the Arabic emphatic consonants ص (ṣād), ض (ḍād), ط (ṭā), and ظ (ẓā) are usually represented by placing one dot under their non-emphatic counterparts, (ṣ, ḍ, ṭ, and ẓ).

NON EMPHATIC				EMPHATIC			
sīn	س	=	s	ṣād	ص	=	ṣ
dāl	د	=	d	ḍād	ض	=	ḍ
tā	ت	=	t	ṭā	ط	=	ṭ
zay	ز	=	z	ẓā	ظ	=	ẓ

2. The throat consonants are represented as follows:

hamza	ء	' (an apostrophe)
hā	ح	ḥ
khā	خ	kh
‘ain	ع	‘ (a single quotation mark)
ghain	غ	gh
hā	ه	h

When kh (ﺥ) occurs with underlining (<u>kh</u>), it is used for one letter <u>kh</u>ā (ﺥ). The same convention of underlining (to represent one sound) is also used for letters <u>th</u>ā (ﺙ), <u>dh</u>āl (ﺫ), <u>sh</u>īn (ﺵ) and <u>gh</u>ain (ﻉ).

When there is no underlining, as in kh for example, it represents two different letters kāf (ﻙ) and hā (ﻩ), respectively.

3. The letter rā (ﺭ) and lām (ﻝ) can be pronounced one of the two ways. Therefore, they are transliterated using two different symbols as follows:

— When the letter rā (ﺭ) is pronounced with a 'thick' sound (a sort of velarization), it is known as *taf<u>kh</u>īm* (تَفْخِيمٌ) and it is denoted by an ṙ with a dot over it. To indicate a 'thin' sound of rā, known as *tarqīq* (تَرْقِيقٌ), ordinary English letter r is used.[27]

— In a similar fashion as above, Lām al-Jalālah (لَامُ الْجَلَالَة) with a 'thickening' of sound is transliterated as l with a dot over it (l̇) while English l is used to indicate lām with 'thinning' of sound.

4. Short vowels — fatha, kasra, and ḍamma — are represented by English letters a, i, and u respectively while a dash is placed over them to signify the long vowels: ā, ī, and ū.

5. No distinct symbols are used for nasalized and non-nasalized sounds of the consonant nūn (ﻥ). The reason being that the nasalization or absence of it is a function of *tanwīn* (or nunation) تَنْوِينٌ, *idghām* اِدْغَامٌ, *i<u>kh</u>fā'* إِخْفَاءٌ, *iẓhār* إِظْهَارٌ, and the rules for mīm ﻡ, and nūn ﻥ, etc., which are presented in Chapter Four.

6. The final hā (ﻩ) preceded by a short vowel, *fatha*, is scarcely pronounced except in the word Allah اَللّٰه. Hence, it is written Sūra, Fatiha, Hijra, etc., where the Arabic spelling would require Sūrah, Fatihah, Hijrah, respectively.

---

[27] See Chapter Four for detailed discussion.

TABLE 1: TRANSLITERATION TABLE OF ARABIC ALPHABET

No	Consonants	Name	Transliteration/Pronunciation	
1	ء	hamza	’	as in awful (when strongly emphasized)
2	ا	alif	a	as in all
3	ب	bā	b	as in boy
4	ت	tā	t	soft sound of t as in theatre or as pronounced by an Italian
5	ث	thā	th	as in think
6	ج	jīm	j	as in John
7	ح	ḥā	ḥ	no equivalent English sound*
8	خ	khā	kh	no equivalent sound in English* (strong guttural)
9	د	dāl	d	as in width
10	ذ	dhāl	dh	more emphatic than ‘th’ in that
11	ر	rā	r, ṙ	thin and thick sounds of English r respectively
12	ز	zay	z	as in zoo
13	س	sīn	s	as in sound
14	ش	shīn	sh	as in shallow
15	ص	ṣād	ṣ	as in saw
16	ض	ḍād	ḍ	no equivalent English sound*
17	ط	ṭā	ṭ	no equivalent English sound*
18	ظ	ẓā	ẓ	no equivalent English sound*
19	ع	‘ain	‘	no equivalent English sound*
20	غ	ghain	gh	a sort of gargling sound as in ghoul
21	ف	fā	f	as in fox
22	ق	qāf	q	no equivalent English sound*
23	ك	kāf	k	as in king
24	ل	lām	l, ĺ	thin and thick sound of English l respectively
25	م	mīm	m	as in moon
26	ن	nūn	n	as in noon, or as in uncle (nasal sound)

27	ه	hā	h	as in heat
28	و	waw	w	as in walk (with *ḥaraka*) as in fool (when *sākin*)
29	ي	yā	y	as in yard (beginning sound) as in speed (middle sound)

* See Chapter Three on "Places and Manners of Articulation" for correct pronunciation

TABLE 1: TRANSLITERATION OF ARABIC VOWELS

SHORT VOWELS		SYMBOL	VOWEL SOUND	ARABIC EXAMPLE	
Fatha	ـَ	a	as in polar	Lan	لَنْ
Kasra	ـِ	i	as in sin	Jinn	جِنْ
Ḍamma	ـُ	u	as in put	Kun	كُنْ

LONG VOWELS

ـَ + ا		ā	as in father	Lā	لَا
ـِ + ي		ī	as in me	Lī	لِي
ـُ + و		ū	as in rule	Nūr	نُورٌ

DIPHTHONGS

ـَ + ي		ai	as in paid	Saifun	سَيْفٌ
ـَ + و		au	as in taught	Khaufun	خَوْفٌ

THE ORGANS OF SPEECH

The traditional method of describing speech sound is in terms of the movements of the vocal organs that produce them. The main organs that are important in the production of speech are the lungs, the windpipe, the larynx (containing the vocal cords), the throat or pharynx, the nose, and the mouth. A diagram of these vocal organs is given in Figure 1.

The source of energy for speech production is the steady stream of air that comes from the lungs. During speech, the air stream is set into vibration by the vocal cord's action. The vocal cords are a part of the larynx. They constitute an adjustable barrier across the air passage coming from the lungs. When the vocal cords are open, the air stream passes into the vocal tract; when closed, they shut off the air flow from the lungs. During speech, the vocal cords open and close rapidly and the shape of the vocal tract is altered by movement of the tongue, the lips, etc., thus producing the different sounds of speech.

The mechanism just described is used for producing most speech sounds. Two other methods are available to produce sound. In one, the vocal tract is constricted at some point along its length. The air stream passing through the constriction becomes turbulent (just like steam escaping through the narrow nozzle of a boiling tea kettle). This turbulent air stream sounds like a hiss and is, in fact, the hissy or "fricative" noise produced when sounds like 's' or 'sh' is produced. The other method is to stop the flow of air altogether momentarily by blocking the vocal tract with the tongue or lips and then suddenly releasing the air pressure built up behind the block. The use of the "blocking" technique to produce sounds like 'b' and 'p' is called "plosive."

At the top of the larynx is the pear shaped epiglottis. While swallowing, the epiglottis helps to deflect food away from the windpipe (or trachea), performing part of the larynx's valve function. The valve action of the larynx depends largely on the vocal cords. The space between the vocal cords is called the glottis. When the arytenoids — and, therefore, the vocal cords — are pressed together, the air passage is completely sealed off and the laryngeal valve is shut. The glottal opening can be controlled by moving the aryteniods apart, as shown in Figure 2.

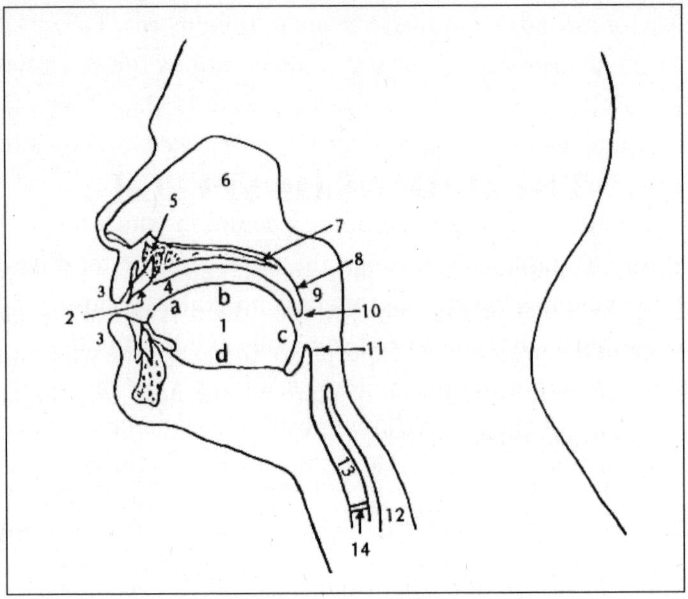

FIGURE 1: The Organs of Speech

1. Tongue: (a) Blade (b) Front (c) Back (d) Root, 2. Tooth, 3. Lips, 4. Oral (mouth) Cavity, 5. Alveolar Ridge (teeth ridge), 6. Nasal Cavity, 7. Hard Palate, 8. Soft Palate, 9. Pharyngeal Cavity, 10. Uvula, 11. Epiglottis, 12. Esophagus (food pipe), 13. Trachea (wind pipe or throat), 14. Vocal Cords

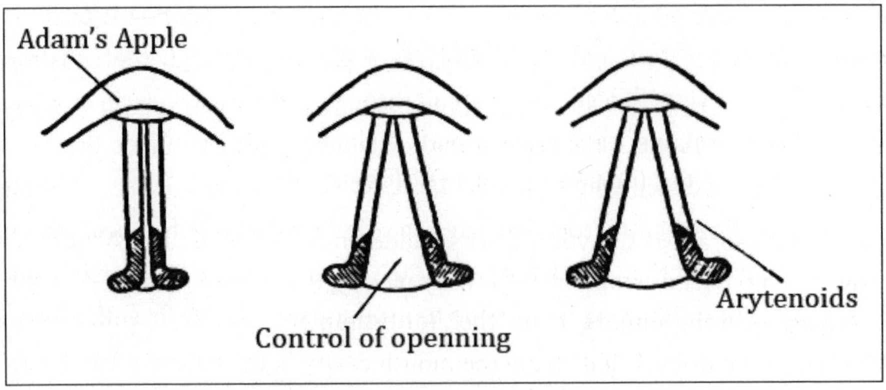

FIGURE 2: The control of the glottal opening.
The shaded areas represent the arytenoids. The curved, top portion of the figure is the Adam's apple.

The pharynx is part of the vocal tract nearest to the glottis. It is a tube connecting the larynx with the mouth and the nose. At its lower end, the pharynx meets the larynx and the esophagus and its wider upper end joins with the back of the mouth and the nose as shown in Figure 1.

The nasal cavity extends from the pharynx to the nostrils. The nasal cavity can be isolated from the pharynx and the back of the mouth by the soft palate or uvula. The soft palate may be raised forming a velic closure in the upper pharynx; or it may be lowered, allowing air to pass through the nose. The two possibilities may be distinguished by calling the accompanying sounds either oral or nasal. A common practice, however, is to use the term *nasal* for a sound in which the oral passage is blocked and all the air passes out through the nose, and the term *nasalized* for a sound in which the velum is lowered but there is no oral stop closure, so that some of the air passes out through the nose and some through the mouth.

The last and most important part of the vocal tract is the mouth. Its shape and size can be varied by adjusting the relative positions of the palate, the tongue, the lips and the teeth. The most flexible of these is the tongue. Its tip, its edge, and its center can be moved independently; the entire tongue can move backward, forward, and up and down.

The lips, which affect both the length and shape of the vocal tract, can be rounded or spread to various degrees, as shown in Figure 3. They can also be closed to stop the air flow altogether.

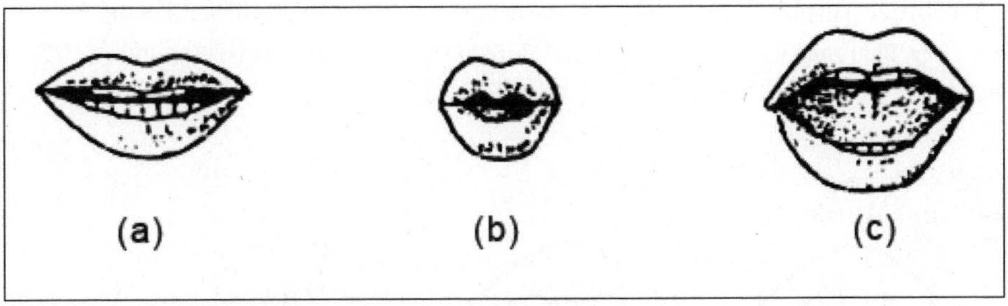

FIGURE 3: The shapes of the lips during articulation:
(a) spread, (b) rounded, (c) unrounded

The teeth also affect the vocal tract's shape and the sounds it produces. They can be used to restrict or stop the air flow by placing them close to the lips or the tip of the tongue, as in the sounds "v" or "the", for example.

The last of the organs that shape the mouth cavity is the palate. It can be divided into three parts:

a. teeth-ridge (alveolus), covered by gums,
b. the bony hard palate, forming roof of the mouth,
c. the muscular soft palate at the back.

The above description of the organs of speech will be extremely helpful in articulating the sound of the Arabic letters as presented in the following section.

THE PLACES AND MANNERS OF ARTICULATION

There are seventeen points at which the basic Arabic sounds are articulated; however, no attempt would be made here to give a detailed description of these seventeen points of articulation. Instead, the sounds are grouped together for the sake of simplicity and intended use of the material for Non-Arabic speakers as well as for the beginners. If the reader desires a detailed exposition of the matter, some useful references are included at the end of the book for appropriate material.

The Arabic sounds are grouped into the following three main categories:

A. Oral cavity (vowel) sounds,

B. Nasal cavity (*ghunna* غُنَّة) sounds,

C. Consonantal sounds.

A classification of all Arabic vowels, nasals, and consonants, according to their places and manners of articulation, is given in Figure 4, Chart 2, and Table 2.

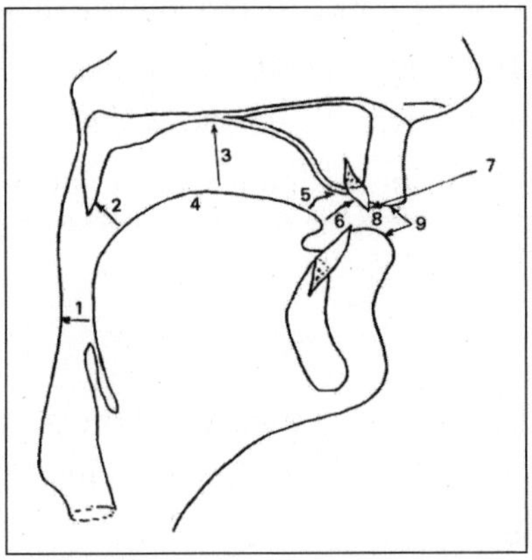

FIGURE 4: Places of Articulation

1. Pharyngeal (throat) consonants (ء، ه، ح، ع، خ، غ)
2. Uvular consonants (ك ، ق)
3. Palatal consonants (ج ، ش ، ي)
4. Molar consonant (ض)
5. Alveolar consonants (ر ، ل ، ن)
6. Dental consonants (ت ، د ، ط)
7. Alveo-dental consonants (ث ، ذ ، ظ)
8. Inter-dental consonants (ز ، س ، ص)
9. Labial consonants (ب ، ف ، م ، و)

A. ORAL CAVITY SOUNDS (VOWELS): The short vowels (*ḍamma*, *fatha*, and *kasra*) were explained in Chapter Two. They are articulated from the oral or mouth cavity.

B. NASAL CAVITY SOUNDS (NASALIZATION): The nasal sounds of nūn and mīm (for observing *ikhfā'* and *idghām*) are pronounced by passing air partially or completely from the nasal cavity. The nasalization of nūn and mīm is a quality which will be discussed in detail in Chapter Four.

C. CONSONANTAL SOUNDS: The twenty eight Arabic consonants are grouped together into the following nine categories (see Figure 4 above):

1. PHARYNGEAL (THROAT) CONSONANTS (غ ، خ ، ع ، ح ، هـ ، ء)

The following six consonants known as the "throat" consonants are foreign to English. They are pronounced from three different points of articulation in the throat: upper throat, middle throat, and lower part of the throat.[28]

a. LOWER THROAT: hamza (ء) and hā (هـ)

Hamza (ء) is a click produced by a quick compression of the lower part of the throat which is closer to the chest. Phonetically, it is referred to as "glottal stop."

Hā (هـ) is produced in the back of the throat. Phonetically, it is referred to as voiceless glottal spirant. It is much like the English Letter 'h'.

b. MIDDLE THROAT: ḥā (ح) and ʻain (ع)

Ḥā (ح) is pronounced with a strong expulsion of air from the chest using middle of the throat. It is a hard guttural or throat sound, more aspirated than hā (هـ). A common practice is to pronounce this sound as that of hā (هـ). Care should be taken to avoid such a substitution of ح by هـ.

'Ain (ع) is a very strong guttural produced by compression of air passages deep down in the throat and expulsion of the breath. The 'ain is similar to the sound one produces sometimes to express the feeling of being strangled. 'Ain carries an echo which can be clearly heard if one closes one's ear when pronouncing the sound of 'ain.

Note that ḥā (ح) and 'ain (ع) are pairs; they differ in that ḥā (ح) has a "hoarseness" without which it would sound like 'ain (ع).

c. UPPER THROAT: khā (خ) and ghain (غ)

Khā (خ) is a strongly marked continuous guttural, produced at the back of the palate, not existing in English but heard in the Scottish "lock" and the German "lochen" but more from the part of the throat closer to the tongue.

Ghain (غ) has a hard sound between a snarling pronunciation of 'gh' and 'r'. It is like the French guttural 'r' strongly uttered through the hard palate, as in the French-pronunciation of the word Paris ("Paghis"). The nearest to it in English is the sound of 'gh' in "ghoul." Ghain (غ) is also similar to the sound made in gargling.

[28] It is recommended that the readers should learn correct pronunciation of these letters from an expert or a native speaker.

2. UVULAR CONSONANTS (ق , ك)

These two uvular consonants are formed with the back of tongue touching or near the soft palate close to uvula.

Qāf (ق): Its proper sound is uttered by forced expulsion of the breath through the soft palate.

Kāf (ك): It is articulated at the part of the tongue just below the point of articulation of qāf ق and the part of the palate directly above it.

The reader must take extreme care in distinguishing the sound of ق from that of ك. It can cause confusion in meaning if not properly pronounced. For example:

Qalbun قَلْبٌ (which means "a heart")
Kalbun كَلْبٌ (which means "a dog")

3. PALATAL CONSONANTS (ج , ش , ي)

These are palatal or oral cavity consonants. They are articulated at the mid-tongue, half way between it and the center of the palate.

Jīm (ج) : The accepted sound of ج is the sound of 'j' in the English word "John." It should not be pronounced as the hard 'g' as in "good."

Yā (ي) : It is pronounced as in the English word "yeast." When used with Waw (و), care should be taken to retain the consonantal sound in diphthong.

Shīn (ش) : This is equivalent to the English sound of 'sh' as in "shot" or "shy."

4. MOLAR CONSONANT (ض)

The sound of the letter ḍād (ض) is foreign to English and can only be pronounced with the help of a native Arabic speaker. It is pronounced by the side of the tongue touching the left or right molars. It is easier to pronounce it from the left side (left side of the tongue and left molars) than the right side. Under no circumstances should it be pronounced like dāl (د).

5. ALVEOLAR CONSONANTS (ر , ل , ن)

The alveolar consonants are articulated with the tip of the tongue touching or near the alveolar ridge or teeth ridge.

Nūn (ن): It is articulated at a point by placing tongue a little above the incisors.

Rā (ر): Unlike the English 'r', it is trilled with the tip of the tongue rapidly touching the alveolar ridge. The tip of the tongue is not curled.

Lām (ل): This is equivalent to the English lateral consonant 'l'. It is made by putting the tip of the tongue against the upper gums and allowing the air to pass on either side of the tongue.

Note: There are two types of ل and ر sounds:[29]

(a) *TAFKHĪM*: where ل or ر is pronounced with a 'thick' sound, a sort of velarization that accompanies the particular phoneme.

(b) *TARQĪQ*: opposes tafkhīm to indicate a 'thin' sound that is to be pronounced without velarization of any kind.

6. DENTAL CONSONANTS (ط , د , ت)

The dental consonants are pronounced with the tongue against the upper teeth.

The letter tā (ت) and dāl (د) are closer in pronunciation to the Italian dental 't' and d' than the English sound. They are uttered with the tip of the tongue against the upper teeth, i.e., at the bases of the incisors.

The letter ṭā (ط) should not be pronounced as tā (ت). It is pronounced with the tip of the tongue behind the lower teeth, with the blade of the tongue behind the upper teeth touching the gums.

7. ALVEO-DENTAL CONSONANTS (ظ , ذ , ث)

The alveo-dentals of thā (ث), dhāl (ذ), and ẓā (ظ) are pronounced with the tip of the tongue touching the edges of the upper front teeth (incisors) as in the English word "think" and "that," respectively. It should be noted that the Arabic pronunciation is more emphatic than the English.

The letter ẓā (ظ) is also foreign to English. It is pronounced in such a way that the tip of the tongue points to the upper lip, ẓā (ظ) is pronounced with more stress than zay (ز).

8. INTER-DENTAL CONSONANTS (ص , س , ز)

The letters sīn (س) and zay (ز) are more sibilant than in English. The sīn (س) is a strong clear sound as 'hissing' to be sharply differentiated from the emphatic ṣād (ص), the tip of the tongue is behind the upper teeth. The letter zay (ز) is a clear buzzing sound as in 'whizzing'.

The letter ṣād (ص) is pronounced with the blade of the tongue against the teeth-ridge, the tip being behind the lower teeth. Observe the thickness of the voice

---

[29] See Chapter Four for detailed discussion and explanation.

in pronouncing the English word 'saw' and compare it with the thinness of the voice in 'see.'

9. LABIAL CONSONANTS (و , م , ف , ب)

The letters in this category are grouped together since they are all formed using labial (lip), bilabial (both lips), labio-dental (lips and teeth), and so on.

The labial consonants are pronounced more or less as their English equivalents. It should be observed, however, that waw (و), when having a *sukūn* and ending on a syllable, should still be pronounced as a consonant, with the lips rounded and protruding.

The letters bā (ب), mīm (م), and waw (و) are formed using both lips (bilabial) while fā (ف) is a labio-dental fricative, i.e., the back part of the lower lip and the edge of the higher front incisors are used.

CHART NO. 2 : THE PLACES OF ARTICULATION

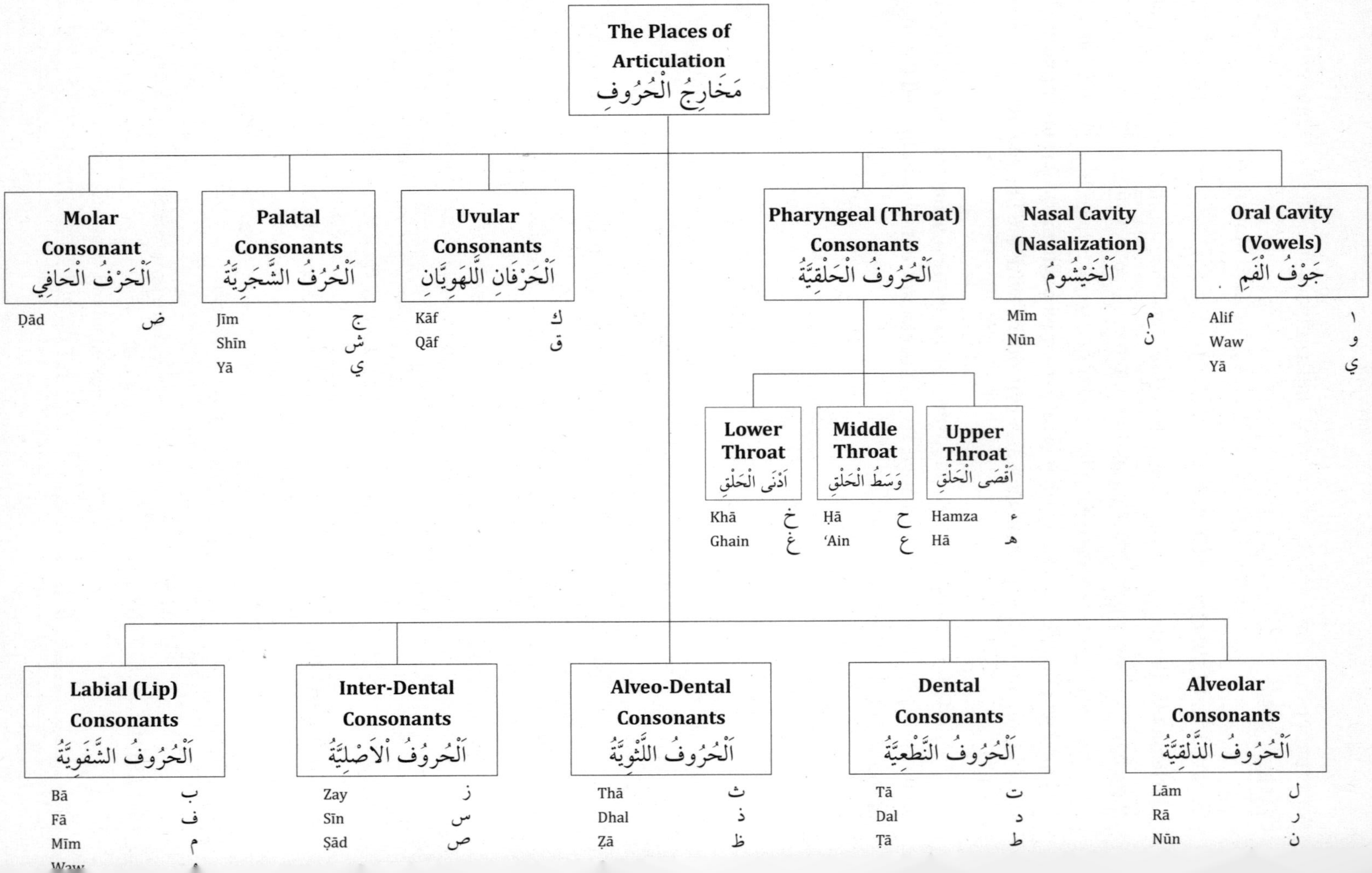

TABLE 2: THE PLACES AND MANNERS OF ARTICULATION

Places of Articulation	Arabic Letters	Manner of Articulation
1. THROAT اَلْحَلْقِيَّةُ	a) ء , ه b) ح , ع c) خ , غ	Foreign to English Pronounced from different parts of the throat: a) Lower b) Middle c) Upper
2. UVULAR اَللَّهَوِيَّانِ	a) ك b) ق	a) Pronounced with the back of the tongue touching or near the soft palate close to uvula b) Foreign to English
3. PALATAL اَلشَّجَرِيَّةُ	a) ج b) ش c) ي	Pronounced in the oral cavity at mid-tongue position half-way between tongue and center of the palate
4. MOLAR اَلْحَافِي	a) ض	Foreign to English Pronounced with the side of the tongue touching left or right molars
5. ALVEOLAR اَلذَّلْقِيَّةُ	a) ل b) ر c) ن	Pronounced with the tip of the tongue touching or near the teeth-ridge (alveolar ridge)
6. DENTAL اَلنَّطْعِيَّةُ	a) ت b) د c) ط	a) & b) are pronounced with the tongue against upper teeth c) Is foreign to English
7. ALVEO-DENTAL اَللَّثَوِيَّةُ	a) ث b) ذ c) ظ	Foreign to English Pronounced with the tip of the tongue touching the edges of the upper front teeth (incisors)
8. INTER-DENTAL اَلْاَصْلِيَّةُ	a) ز b) س c) ص	Produced with whistling (hissing) a) & b) are pronounced with the tip of the tongue behind upper teeth c) is pronounced with the blade of the tongue against the teeth-ridge, the tip being behind the lower teeth
9. LABIAL اَلشَّفَوِيَّةُ	a) ب b) ف c) م d) و	a), b) & c) are pronounced using both lips (bilabial) d) is pronounced using back part of the lower lip and the edge of the front upper teeth (incisors)

Chapter Four

THE RULES OF TAJWĪD

CHART NO. 3: THE RULES OF THE LETTERS

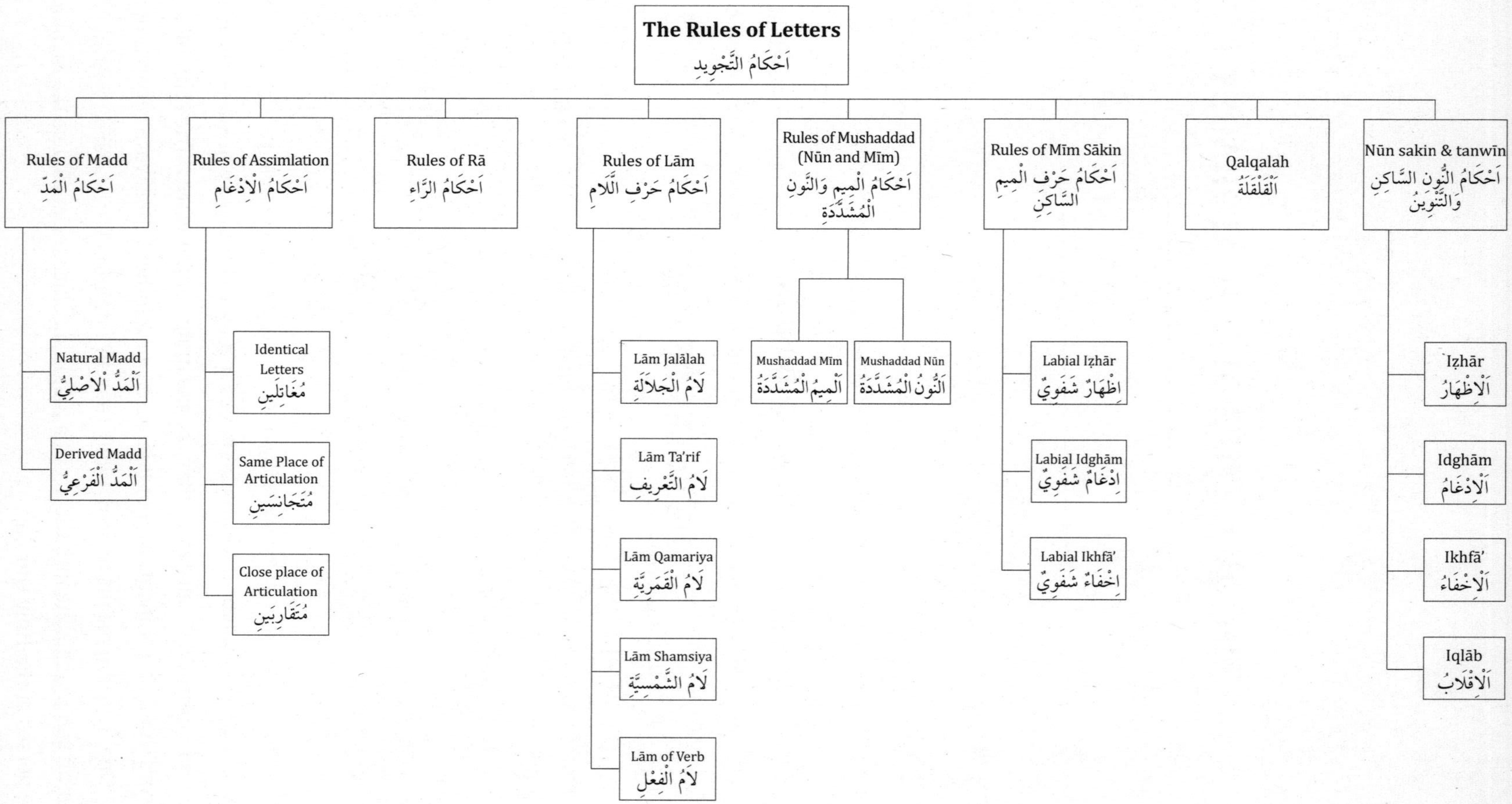

THE QUALITIES OF THE ALPHABET

صِفَاتُ الْحُرُوفِ

Tajwīd means to pronounce each Arabic letter correctly from its proper place of articulation (مَخْرَجٌ) and with all its qualities (صِفَاتٌ). In the previous chapter, the topic of manner and places of articulation was covered in detail. Here, the qualities of the letters will be discussed.

The way in which a letter with its distinct quality is pronounced is called *Sifat al-Huruf* (صِفَاتُ الْحُرُوفِ). The examples of such qualities are letters pronounced softly, sharply, with an abrupt ending, with a soft ending, with thin or thick sound, etc.

There are two most common errors made by the readers during the pronunciation of the Arabic alphabet:

1. CLEAR ERRORS (اَلَّحْنُ الْجَلِيُّ): In this case the error is so obvious or clear that it changes the meanings of the words altogether. They are the result of any one the following:

(a) substituting one letter for another one: ثَمَدٌ for صَمَدٌ
قَلْبٌ for كَلْبٌ

(b) adding an additional letter to a word: اَنَا or اَنْ

(c) dropping a letter from a word: كَتَبُوا for كَتَبَ
or اَخَذْنَ for اَخَذْنَا

(d) changing of vowel sounds (*fatha, kasra, ḍamma*) or *sukūn*:
عَلِمْتُ (I knew) for عَلِمْتَ (you knew, for male) or عَلِمْتِ (you knew, for female).

All of the above mistakes alter the meanings of the words. The examples of the errors due to the substitution of one letter for another letter were covered in Chapter One. It is important to remember that an intentional or careless reading of the Qur'an can plunge one into the act of a major sin since it can change the meanings of the verses of the Holy Qur'an.

2. MINOR ERRORS (اَللَّحْنُ الْخَفِيُّ): When the letters are pronounced with their right qualities, they add beauty to the sound of words. For example, the letter ر and ل are pronounced either with a "full mouth" (heavy voice) called *tafkhīm* or with an "empty mouth" (thin voice) called *tarqīq*, depending upon the preceding vowel. A failure to observe these qualities of the letters will lead to some "minor errors." Although these errors are not as severe as in case of "clear errors," they are strongly discouraged for a correct and beautiful recitation of the Qur'an.

The qualities of the alphabet are shown in Table 3 and 4 and a detailed explanation with examples is presented in the following pages.

TABLE 3: THE QUALITIES OF THE LETTERS (WITH OPPOSITES)

No	Basic Quality	Letters	Opposite Quality	Letters
1.	WEAK/LOW اَلْهَمْسُ	ف / ح / ث / ه ش / خ / ص س / ك / ت	STRONG/HIGH اَلْجَهْرُ	the rest of the alphabet
2.	FORCEFUL/HARD اَلشِّدَّةُ	ا / ج / د ق / ط ب / ك / ت	SOFT اَلرَّخَاوَةُ	the rest of the alphabet
3.	ELEVATED اَلْاِسْتِعْلَاءُ	خ / ص ض / غ / ط ق / ظ	DEPRESSED اَلْاِسْتِفَالُ	the rest of the alphabet
4.	CLOSED/ROUNDED اَلْاِطْبَاقُ	ص / ض ط / ظ	OPEN اَلْاِنْفِتَاحُ	the rest of the alphabet
5.	SWIFTLY FLOWING اَلْاِذْلَاقُ	ف / ر م / ن ل / ب	SHARP اَلْاِصْمَاتُ	the rest of the alphabet

TABLE 4: THE QUALITIES OF THE LETTERS (NO OPPOSITES)

No	Basic Quality		Letters
1.	WHISTLING	اَلصَّفِيرُ	ز / س / ص
2.	ECHOING	اَلْقَلْقَلَةُ	ق / ط / ب / ج / د
3.	PROLONGED	اَلْمَدُّ	ا / و / ي
4.	SOFT	اَللِّينُ	ـَ وْ / ـَ يْ
5.	BENDING	اَلْاِنْحِرَافُ	ل / ر
6.	VIBRATING	اَلتَّكْرِيرُ	ر
7.	EXPANDING	اَلتَّفَشِّيُّ	ش
8.	ELONGATED	اَلْاِسْتِطَالَةُ	ض
9.	MODERATED	اَلتَّوَسُّطُ	ل / ن / ع / م / ر
10.	NASALIZED	اَلْغُنَّةُ	م / ن

Note: Most authorities do not consider Prolonged (*al-Madd* اَلْمَدُّ), Moderated (*al-Mutawassita* اَلْمُتَوَسِّطَةُ), and Nasalized (*al-Ghunna* اَلْغُنَّةُ) as a separate quality. According to them, these qualities are not permanent but rather occur only when certain conditions occur such as *Madd*, *Idghām*, *lkhfā*, and so on.

THE RULES OF NŪN SĀKIN AND TANWĪN

اَحْكَامُ النُّونِ السَّاكِنِ وَالتَّنْوِينِ

The letter ن with a sukūn, indicating absence of a vowel sign (اَلْحَرَكَةُ), is called *nūn sākin* (نْ). *Tanwīn* means to produce the sound of ن and it is expressed by a double fatha (ـً) (اَلْفَتْحَتَيْنِ), double kasra (ـٍ) (اَلْكَسْرَتَيْنِ), and double ḍamma (ـٌ) (اَلضَّمَّتَيْنِ). There are four rules regarding the pronunciation of *nūn sākin* and *tanwīn* as follows:

A.	IZHĀR	اَلْاِظْهَارُ :	A clear or sharp pronunciation without nasalization (اَلْغُنَّةُ) and prolongation (اَلْمَدُّ).
B.	IDGHĀM	اَلْاِدْغَامُ :	A partial or complete assimilation of one letter into another with or without nasalization.
C.	IKHFĀ'	اَلْاِخْفَاءُ :	A slight nasal sound, half way between *iẓhār* and *idghām*.
D.	IQLĀB	اَلْاِقْلَابُ :	Change of *nūn sākin* of *tanwīn* by the letter م when followed by the letter ب.

Each of the above quality of *nūn sākin* and *tanwīn* is presented in the following pages of this chapter.

A. IZHĀR (اَلْاِظْهَارُ)

Izhār means to express clearly and sharply. In tajwīd, if after *nūn sākin* or *tanwīn* there is a letter from the six throat consonants, then the sound of *nūn* (in *nūn sākin* or *tanwīn*) will be pronounced clear and sharp without nasalization (غُنَّة) and without any lengthening (مَدّ). The six throat consonants, as discussed in Chapter Three, are as follows:

hamza	ء	and	hā	هـ
'ain	ع	and	ḥā	ح
ghain	غ	and	khā	خ

For *Izhār*, the following three conditions must be satisfied:

1. There must appear one of the six throat consonants after *nūn sākin* or *tanwīn*.
2. *Nūn sākin* appears in verbs, nouns, and prepositions. It is either in the middle or at the end of a word. *Izhār* of *nūn sākin* may occur in one word (if *nūn sākin* is in the middle of the word) or in two words (if *nūn sākin* is at the end of the first word).
3. *Tanwīn* (double ḍamma, double fatha and double kasra) occurs in nouns only. For *Izhār* of *tanwīn*, two words are required; *tanwīn* should be at the end of the first word and the second word must begin with one of the throat consonants.

Izhār of *nūn sākin* can occur in one word or two words:

One word:	عَنْهُمْ	*nūn sākin* within the word
		letter of *Izhār* (هـ) follows *nūn sākin*

Two words:	مِنْ خَوْفٍ	first word with *nūn sākin* at the end
		second word begins with a letter of *Izhār* (خ)

Izhār of *tanwīn* can occur only in two words:	مِنْ خَوْفٍ	first word ends with tanwīn (double ḍamma ٌ)
		second word begins with a letter of *Izhār* (ح)

EXAMPLES:

1. IZHĀR OF NŪN SĀKIN

NO.	LETTER OF IZHĀR	IZHĀR IN TWO WORDS	IZHĀR IN ONE WORD
1.	Hamza ء	مِنْ اٰلِهٖ	يَنْئَوْنَ
2.	Hā هـ	اِنْ هٰذَا	عَنْهُمْ
3.	'Ain ع	مِنْ عَذَابٍ	اَنْعَمْتَ
4.	Ḥā ح	مِنْ حَيْثُ	يَنْحِتُوْنَ
5.	Ghain غ	مِنْ غَيْرِ	فَسَيُنْغِضُوْنَ
6.	Khā خ	وَاِنْ خِفْتُمْ	وَالْمُنْخَنِقَةُ

2. IZHĀR OF TANWĪN

NO.	LETTER OF IZHĀR		IZHĀR OF DOUBLE KASRA (ٍ)	IZHĀR OF DOUBLE FATHA (ً)	IZHĀR OF DOUBLE ḌAMMA (ٌ)
1.	Hamza	ء	بِمَعْرُوفٍ اَوْ	مَرَّةً اُخْرَى	فِتْنَةٌ اَوْ
2.	Hā	هـ	قَوْمٍ هَادٍ	فَرِيقًا هَدَى	سَلاَمٌ هِيَ
3.	‘Ain	ع	بِغَافِلٍ عَمَّا	اَجْرًا عَظِيماً	قَوِيٌّ عَزِيزٌ
4.	Ḥā	ح	بِقَوْمٍ حَتَّى	رِزْقًا حَسَنًا	غَنِيٌّ حَمِيدٌ
5.	Ghain	غ	اِلٰهٍ غَيْرُهُ	زَوْجًا غَيْرَهُ	عَزِيزٌ غَفُورٌ
6.	Khā	خ	يَوْمَئِذٍ خَاشِعَةٌ	نَارًا خَالِدًا	عَلِيمٌ خَبِيرٌ

B. IDGHĀM (اَلْإِدْغَامُ)

Idghām means to contract, to merge, to assimilate, or to join. In tajwīd, *idghām* of *nūn sākin* or *tanwīn* means to merge *nūn sākin* or *tanwīn* into the first letter of the following word.

If after *nūn sākin* or *tanwīn*, there appears in the following word one of the six letters of *idghām* (ن, و, ل, م, ر, ي = يَرْمِلُونَ) then the *nūn sākin* or *tanwīn* will be assimilated into this letter.

Idghām is also possible when there is no *nūn sākin* or *tanwīn*. It will be covered later in this chapter on Rules of Sākin Mīm, Mushaddad Mīm and Mushaddad Nūn.

For *idghām* of *nūn sākin* and *tanwīn*, the following two conditions must be satisfied:

1. There should be two consecutive words; *idghām* never occurs with one word alone.
2. The *nūn sākin* or *tanwīn* must be at the end of the first word and the second word begins with one of the letter of *idghām* (ن, و, ل, م, ر, ي).

There are two types of *idghām*:

1. Partial merger with nasalization
2. Complete merger without nasalization

1. PARTIAL MERGER WITH NASALIZATION (اِدْغَامُ النَّاقِص مَعَ الْغُنَّة)

In Partial Merger, the sound of *nūn sākin* or *tanwīn* is retained in the merging letter to some extent. The conditions for Partial Merger with nasalization are as follows:

(a) Two words, occuring together, are required.

(b) The first word must end with a *sākin nūn* or *tanwīn*.

(c) The second word must begin with any of the four letters of partial *idghām* و, ن, م, ي. These letters of *idghām* can he remembered by the word يَمْنُو containing them.

(d) The letter of *idghām* (و, ن, م, ي) becomes mushaddad and is pronounced as one word. The mushaddad letter is nasalized equal to two *ḥaraka*.

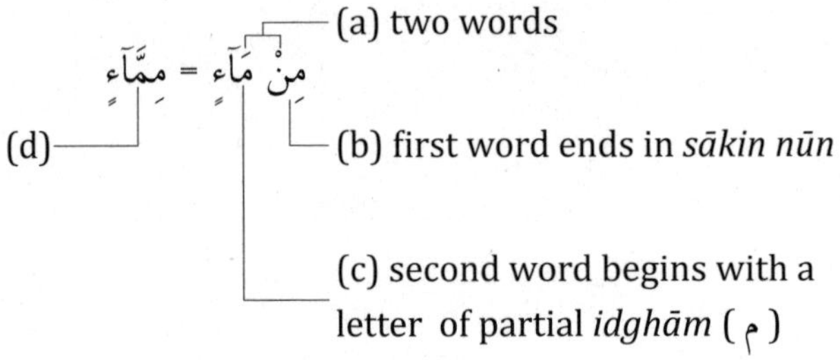

Pronunciation: *Nūn sākin* in مِنْ is merged into م of مَآء and the two words are pronounced as one word مِمَّآءٍ with nasalization of mushaddad mīm equal to a length of two *ḥaraka*.

EXAMPLES:

(a) PARTIAL MERGER OF NŪN SĀKIN (اِدْغَامُ النَّاقِصِ النُّونِ السَّاكِنَةِ)

NO.	LETTER OF PARTIAL IDGHĀM	WRITTEN AS	PRONOUNCED AS (WITH NASALIZATION)
1.	ي	اِنْ يَرَوْا	اِيَّرَوْا
2.	و	مِنْ وَالْ	مِوَّالْ
3.	م	مِنْ مِثْلِهِ	مِمِّثْلِهِ
4.	ن	اِنْ نَقُولُ	اِنَّقُولُ

(b) PARTIAL MERGER OF TANWĪN (اِدْغَامُ النَّاقِصِ التَّنْوِين)

NO.	LETTER OF PARTIAL IDGHĀM	DOUBLE KASRA (ٍ) WRITTEN / PRONOUNCED	DOUBLE FATHA *nūn sākin* or *tanwīn* (ً) WRITTEN / PRONOUNCED	DOUBLE ḌAMMA (ٌ) WRITTEN / PRONOUNCED
1.	ي	لِقَوْمٍ يُؤْمِنُونَ لِقَوْمِيُّؤْمِنُونَ	خَيْرًا يَرَهُ خَيْرَيَّرَهُ	بَرْقٌ يَجْعَلُونَ بَرْقُيَّجْعَلُونَ
2.	و	يَوْمَئِذٍ وَاجِفَةٌ يَوْمَئِذِوَّاجِفَةٌ	اِيْمَانًا وَهُمْ اِيمَانَوَّهُمْ	مَغْفِرَةٌ وَاَجْرٌ مَغْفِرَتُوَّاَجْرٌ
3.	م	بِسُورَةٍ مِنْ بِسُورَتِمِّنْ	صِرَاطًا مُسْتَقِيمًا صِرَاطَمُّسْتَقِيماً	ذُرِّيَّةٌ مِنْ ذُرِّيَّتُمِّنْ
4.	ن	شَيْءٍ نَحْنُ شَيْئِنَّحْنُ	مَلِكًا نُقَاتِلْ مَلِكَنُّقَاتِلْ	حِطَّةٌ نَغْفِرْ لَكُمْ حِطَّتُنَّغْفِرْلَكُمْ

2. COMPLETE MERGER WITHOUT NASALIZATION (اِدْغَامُ النَّاقِصِ مَعَ الْغُنَّةِ)

In Complete Merger, the *nūn sākin* or *tanwīn* disappears as if it never existed. The letter preceding *nūn sākin* or *tanwīn* is connected to the letter after the *nūn sākin* or *tanwīn* in such a way that the letter after the *nūn sākin* or *tanwīn* becomes mushaddad in pronunciation. The conditions for Complete Merger are the same as that of Partial Merger except that the second word must begin with the letter ل or ر _ لْرْ (for memorization purpose.) Complete Merger of *nūn sākin* or *tanwīn* without nasalization cannot occur on any other Arabic letters.

EXAMPLE OF COMPLETE MARGER OF NŪN SĀKIN

(a) two words

مِرَّبِّهِمْ = مِنْ رَبِّهِمْ

(d)

(b) first word ends in *sākin nūn*

(c) second word begins with one of the letters of Complete Merger (ر)

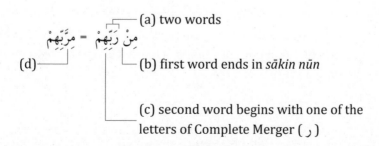

Pronunciation: *Nūn sākin* in مِنْ is completely merged into ر of رَبِّهِمْ and the two words are pronounced as one without nasalization مِرَّبِّهِمْ.

EXAMPLES:

(a) COMPLETE MERGER OF NŪN SĀKIN (اِدغامُ التَّامِ النُّونِ السَّاكِنَةِ)

NO.	LETTER OF COMPLETE MERGER	WRITTEN AS	PRONOUNCED AS (WITHOUT NASALIZATION)
1.	ل	اَنْ لَوْ	اَلَّوْ
2.	ر	مِنْ رَبِّ	مِرَّبِّ

(b) COMPLETE MERGER OF NŪN TANWĪN (اِدغَامُ التَّامِ التَّنْوِينِ)

NO.	LETTER OF COMPLETE MERGER	DOUBLE KASRA (ٍ) PRONOUNCED / WRITTEN	DOUBLE FATHA (ً) PRONOUNCED / WRITTEN	DOUBLE ḌAMMA (ٌ) PRONOUNCED / WRITTEN
1.	ل	يَوْمَئِذٍ لَخَبِيرٌ يَوْمَئِذِلَّخَبِيرٌ	اَنْدَادًا لِيُضِلُّوا اَنْدَادَلِّيُضِلُّوا	خَيْرٌ لِلَّذِينَ خَيْرُلِّلَّذِينَ
2.	ر	رَبٍّ رَحِيمٍ رَبِّرَّحِيمٍ	تَوَّابًا رَحِيمًا تَوَّابَرَّحِيمًا	غَفُورٌ رَحِيمٌ غَفُورُرَّحِيمٌ

EXCEPTIONS

The following are exceptions to the rules of *idghām* of *nūn sākin* and *tanwīn*:

1. There are two places in the Qur'an where *iẓhār* is always observed even though they appear to satisfy the conditions of *idghām* of *nūn sākin*. The two exceptions are as follows:

يٰسٓ ۞ وَالْقُرْآنِ الْحَكِيمِ (36: 1-2)

نٓ وَالْقَلَمِ وَمَا يَسْطُرُونَ (68: 1)

A close examination here would reveal that Yā-Sīn (يٰسٓ) and Nūn (نٓ) do not satisfy a necessary condition for *idghām* of having two words. Yā-Sīn (يٰسٓ) and Nūn (نٓ) are not words; they are letters known as Abbreviated Letters[30] (اَلْحُرُوفُ الْمُقَطَّعَاتُ). The يٰسٓ are two letters ي and س while ن is one letter; therefore, no Partial *idghām* occurs in both cases.

2. At the following two places in the Holy Qur'an, *idghām* is not observed although they satisfy the conditions of Complete Merger:

بَلْ ۜ رَانَ (83: 14)

وَقِيلَ مَنْ ۜ رَاقٍ (75: 27)

Idghām can only occur in continuous recitation. Due to a pause,[31] indicated by a small س in between the two words, continuous recitation is not possible.

3. As mentioned earlier, *idghām* occurs with two words. The following words are pronounced without *idghām*:

دُنْيَا (2: 85)

قِنْوَانٌ (6: 99)

صِنْوَانٌ (13: 4)

بُنْيَانٌ (61: 4)

The above words are pronounced with absolute *iẓhār* known as اَلْاِظْهَارُ الْمُطْلَقُ.

C. IKHFĀ (اَلْإِخْفَاءُ)

Ikhfā' means to conceal, to hide, or to cover. In tajwīd, if after *nūn sakīn* or *tanwīn* there appears any letter (except the six throat consonants of *iẓhār*, seven letters of *idghām* and one letter of *iqlāb*), then the sound of nūn in *nūn sakīn* or *tanwīn* is pronounced with a very light sound in the nose and lengthening equal to two *ḥaraka*. The sound of nūn is concealed in such a way that nasal sound (*ghunna*) is partial, i.e., halfway between *iẓhār* and *idghām*.

The difference between Ikhfā and Izhār: Izhār has no nasalization while *ikhfā'* has slight nasalization.

The difference between Ikhfā and idghām: In *idghām*, there is a *tashdīd* on the letter of *idghām* while *ikhfā'* carries no tashdīd on the following letter after *nūn sakīn* or *tanwīn*.

---

30 Refer to Chapter Five for a detailed explanation and discussion about Abbreviated Letters.

31 See *sakta* at the end of this Chapter.

Ikhfā' can be heard in the sound of letter 'n' when the English word 'uncle' is pronounced. Remember that in *ikhfā'* the air passes partially through the nose. To feel vibration in the fingers, hold your nose and pronounce the word 'uncle'.

There are fifteen letters of *ikhfā'*. They are indicated by the first letter of the Arabic words as follows:

1 :	ص	(صَفْ)	6 :	ش	(شَخْصٌ)	11 :	ز	(زِدْ)
2 :	ذ	(ذَا)	7 :	ق	(قَدْ)	12 :	ف	(فِي)
3 :	ث	(ثَنَا)	8 :	س	(سَمَا)	13 :	ت	(تُقًى)
4 :	ك	(كَمْ)	9 :	د	(دُمْ)	14 :	ض	(ضَعْ)
5 :	ج	(جَادَ)	10 :	ط	(طَيِّبًا)	15 :	ظ	(ظَالِمًا)

Ikhfā' of *nūn sakīn* can occur in one word or two words.

One word :	يَنْقَلِبُ	*nūn sakīn*
		one of the letters of *ikhfā'* (ق)
Two words :	مَنْ جَآءَ	first word with *nūn sakīn* at the end
		second word begins with one of the letters of *ikhfā'* (ج)
Ikhfā' of *tanwīn* can occur only in two words:	كِتَابٌ كَبِيرٌ	first word with *tanwīn* (ٌ) at the end.
		second word begins with one of the letters of *ikhfā'* (ك)

EXAMPLES:

1. *Ikhfā'* of *Nūn Sakīn*

NO.	LETTER OF IKHFĀ'	IKHFĀ' IN TWO WORDS	IKHFĀ' IN ONE WORD
1.	Tā : ت	وَاِنْ تَصْبِرُوا	اَنْتَ
2.	Thā : ث	مِنْ ثَمَرِهِ	مَنْثُورًا
3.	Jīm : ج	مِنْ جُوعٍ	اِنْجِيلَ
4.	Dāl : د	مِنْ دُونِ	اَنْدَادًا
5.	Dhāl : ذ	مِنْ ذَلِكَ	تُنْذِرُ
6.	Zā : ز	مِنْ زَقُّومٍ	اَنْزَلَ
7.	Sīn : س	مِنْ سُوءٍ	اِنْسَانٌ
8.	Shīn : ش	فَمَنْ شَآءَ	اَنشَرَهُ
9.	Ṣād : ص	وَلَمَنْ صَبَرَ	اُنْصُرْنَا
10.	Ḍād : ض	لَمَنْ ضَرُّهُ	مَنْضُودٍ
11.	Ṭā : ط	مِنْ طَيِّبَاتٍ	اِنْطَلِقُوا
12.	Ẓā : ظ	مِنْ ظَهِيرٍ	اُنْظُرُوا
13.	Fā : ف	مِنْ فَوْرِهِمْ	يُنْفِقُونَ
14.	Qāf : ق	مِنْ قَبْلِهِمْ	يَنْقَلِبُ
15.	Kāf : ك	وَاِنْ كَانَتْ	مِنْكُمْ

2. *Ikhfā'* of *Tanwīn*

NO.	LETTER OF IKHFĀ'	DOUBLE KASRA (ٍ)	DOUBLE FATHA (ً)	DOUBLE ḌAMMA (ٌ)
1.	Tā : ت	جَنَّاتٍ تَجْرِي	كُلًّا تَبَّرْنَا	حَيَّةٌ تَسْعَى
2.	Thā : ث	نُطْفَةٍ ثُمَّ	شَهِيدًا ثُمَّ	خَيْرٌ ثَوَابًا

3.	Jīm	:	ج	خَلْقٍ جَدِيدٍ	سِرَاجًا جَمِيلاً	فَصَبْرٌ جَمِيلٌ
4.	Dāl	:	د	لِكُلٍّ دَرَجَاتٍ	كَأْسًا دِهَاقًا	ضُرٌّ دَعَانَا
5.	Dhāl	:	ذ	حَقٍّ ذَلِكَ	نَارًا ذَاتَ لَهَبٍ	عَزِيزٌ ذُوانْتِقَامٍ
6.	Zā	:	ز	يَوْمَئِذٍ زُرْقًا	صَعِيداً زَلَقًا	حَمِيدٌ زَعَمَ
7.	Sīn	:	س	شَيْءٍ سَبَبًا	بَشَرًا سَوِيًا	فَوْجٌ سَأَلَهُمْ
8.	Shīn	:	ش	رُكْنٍ شَدِيدٍ	جَبَّارًا شَقِيّاً	لَغَفُورٌ شَكُورٌ
9.	Ṣād	:	ص	بِرِيحٍ صَرْصَرٍ	قَوْمًا صَالِحِينَ	رُكْنٍ شَدِيدٍ
10.	Ḍād	:	ض	قُوَّةٍ ضَعْفًا	قَوْمًا ضَآلِّينَ	ذُرِّيَّةٌ ضُعَفَاءُ
11.	Ṭā	:	ط	كَلِمَةٍ طَيِّبَةٍ	حَلاَلاً طَيِّبًا	قَوْمٌ طَاغُونَ
12.	Ẓā	:	ظ	نَفْسٍ ظُلُمَاتٌ	قَوْمًا ظَالِمِينَ	سَحَابٌ ظُلُمَاتٌ
13.	Fā	:	ف	كَلِمَاتٍ فَتَابَ	مَآءٍ فُرَاتًا	بَيْعٌ فِيهِ
14.	Qāf	:	ق	فِئَةٍ قَلِيلَةٍ	رِزْقًا قَالُوا	فَتْحٌ قَرِيبٌ
15.	Kāf	:	ك	شَيْءٍ كَذَلِكَ	عُلُوًّا كَبِيرًا	اَجْرٌ كَبِيرٌ

D. IQLĀB (اَلْإِقْلاَبُ)

Iqlāb means to change one letter by another one. In tajwīd, if the letter bā (ب) comes after *nūn sakīn* or *tanwīn*, then the *nūn sakīn* or *tanwīn* is replaced by *mīm sākin* (م) and rules of *ikhfā'* are observed in pronunciation. This changing of *nūn sakīn* or *tanwīn* into *sākin mīm* (م) is called *iqlāb*.[32] *Iqlāb* is indicated in the text of the Holy Qur'an by placing a small size mīm (م) over the *nūn sakīn* or *tanwīn*. This cautions the reader that the nūn sound in *nūn sakīn* or *tanwīn* is to be replaced by the letter mīm (م) in pronouncing the word. Note that the letter mīm (م) is always placed close to *nūn sakīn* or *tanwīn* and never on the letter bā (ب) which follows it.

Iqlāb of *nūn sakīn* can be in one word or two words but *iqlāb* of *tanwīn* always requires two words.

---

32 Also known as Qalb.

Iqlāb of Nūn sakīn (one or two words)

PRONOUNCED WRITTEN

nūn sakīn

In one word: اَنْبِيَآءٌ = اَمْبِيَآءٌ

the letter of Iqlāb ب after nūn sakīn

nūn sakīn at the end of the word

In two word: مِنْ بَعْدِ = مِمْبَعْدِ

the letter of Iqlāb ب in the next word

Iqlāb of Tanwīn (two words only)

PRONOUNCED WRITTEN

tanwīn (double damma ــٌ)

سَمِيعٌ بَصِيرٌ = سَمِيعُمْبَصِيرٌ

the letter of Iqlāb ب in the next word

EXAMPLES OF IQLĀB OF NŪN SAKĪN

PRONOUNCED	WRITTEN
اَمْبِئُونِي	اَنْبِئُونِي
مِمْ بَيْنِ	مِنْ بَيْنِ

EXAMPLES OF IQLĀB OF TANWĪN

PRONOUNCED	WRITTEN	TANWĪN
عَوَانُمْ بَيْنَ	عَوَانٌ بَيْنَ	Double ḍamma (ــٌ)
غُرْفَتَمْ بِيَدِهِ	غُرْفَةً بِيَدِهِ	Double fatha (ــً)
شِقَاقِمْ بَعِيدٍ	شِقَاقٍ بَعِيدٍ	Double kasra (ــٍ)

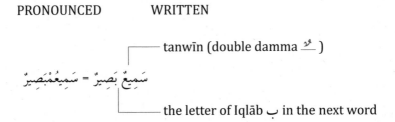

THE QALQALA

اَلْقَلْقَلَةُ

This is a quality of certain letters, which when pronounced, appear to have an echoing sound (pronunciation with a slight vibration in makhraj مَخْرَجُ). Such a vibration is known as *Qalqala* (اَلْقَلْقَلَةُ) in Arabic. This quality is found in the following five letters:

د	ج	ب	ط	ق
dāl	jim	bā	ṭā	qāf

These letters are known as قُطْبُ جَدٍ containing the above five letters of Qalqala.

The letters of Qalqala are divided into three categories according to their intensity as shown in the following table.

CATEGORY	INTENSITY	LETTERS
1	High	Qāf ق
2	Medium	Jīm ج
3	Low	Bā ب
		Dāl د
		Ṭā ط

The Qalqala of qāf is higher in intensity than jīm, and jīm is higher than bā ب, dāl د and ṭā ط. Furthermore, the letters of Qalqala in each category can also be the strongest to weakest in pronunciation depending on whether the letters are *mushaddad* or *sākin* or *mutaḥarrik* (voweled) only if it is in a *sākin* position due to *waqf*, as shown in the following diagram:

STRONGEST	← PRONUNCIATION OF QALQALA →		NO QALQALA
Waqf on Mushaddad letter of Qalqala	Waqf on Qalqala letter when Sākin at the end of the word	Qalqala letter is Sākin in a word (not at the end of the word)	No Qalqala when it has a vowel (ḍamma, fatha or kasra)
EXAMPLES:			
تَبَّتْ يَدَآ اَبِي لَهَبٍ وَتَبَّ Tabbat 111:1 1. Strongest	فَاِذَا فَرَغْتَ فَانْصَبْ Al-Inshirah 94:7 2. Stronger	وَمَآ اُنْزِلَ مِنْ قَبْلِكَ Al-Baqarah 2:4 3. Weakest	وَكَوَاعِبَ اَتْرَابًا An-Naba' 78:33

As shown in the above examples, the Qalqala of bā ب varies in strength from the strongest to weakest: (1) Bā mushaddad with waqf, (2) Bā sākin with waqf, (3) Bā sākin within a word, (4) Bā with ḥaraka (fatha) if stopped (waqf).

The Qalqala has been classified as the Major Qalqala and the Minor Qalqala: The Major Qalqala is when the letter of Qalqala is sākin or mushaddad with waqf at the end of a word. The Minor Qalqala is when the letter of Qalqala is sākin within a word.

EXAMPLES OF MAJOR AND MINOR QALQALA:

NO.	LETTER OF THE QALQALA	MINOR QALQALA قَلْقَلَةُ صُغْرَى	MAJOR QALQALA قَلْقَلَةٌ كُبْرَى
1.	Jīm : ج	يَجْعَلُونَ	مَرِيجْ
2.	Dāl : د	يَدْعُونَ	بَعِيدْ
3.	Qāf : ق	يَقْطَعُونَ	وَاقْ
4.	Ṭā : ط	يَطْمَعُونَ	مُحِيطْ
5.	Bā : ب	لَتُبْلَوُنَّ	عَذَابْ

THE RULES OF LETTER LĀM

اَحْكَامُ حَرْفِ اللاَّمِ

The Rules of Letter Lām ل are as follows.

1. LĀM IN THE GLORIOUS WORD OF ALLAH لَامُ لَفْظِ الْجَلَالَةِ

The mushaddad lām in the word Allah (اَللهُ) or Allahumma (اَللَّهُمَّ) is known as *Lām al-Jalalah*. This lām is pronounced either with a 'full mouth' (heavy, or thick voice) or with an 'empty mouth' (soft or thin voice). The rules that govern pronunciation of *Lām al-Jalalah* with either thick or thin voice are as follows:

a) LĀM AL-JALĀLAH WITH THIN VOICE تَرْقِيقُ اللاَّمِ الْجَلاَلَةِ

If the word Allah (اَللهُ) or Allahumma (اَللَّهُمَّ) is preceded by any letter with kasra, then the *mushaddad lām* will be pronounced softly without the heavy sound of lām. This quality of lām is known as *Lām Tarqīq* (تَرْقِيقُ اللاَّمِ).

EXAMPLES:

بِسْمِ اللهِ

قُلِ اللَّهُمَّ

In the above examples, the word Allah and Allahumma is preceded by mīm with kasra and lām with kasra respectively. Therefore, the letter lām in Allah and Allahumma is pronounced softly with thin voice.

b) LĀM AL-JALĀLAH WITH THICK VOICE تَفْخِيمُ اللاَّمِ الْجَلاَلَةِ

This is opposite of *Tarqīq*. When any letter with fatha or ḍamma appears before the word Allah or Allahumma, the *mushaddad lām* will be pronounced with a heavy, thick, and high pitched sound. This quality of lām is known as *Lām Tafkhīm* (تَفْخِيمُ اللاَّمِ).

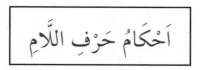

EXAMPLES:

يَعْلَمْهُ اللهُ

اِنَّ اللهَ

قَالُوا اللَّهُمَّ

سُبْحَانَكَ اللَّهُمَّ

Note: With the exception of lām in the Glorious name of Allah or Allahumma, all other lāms are always pronounced thin and soft. For example:

جَعَلْنَا

اِلاَّ

عَلَى

2. LĀM TA'RĪF لَامُ التَّعْرِيفُ

The definite article in Arabic is indicated by "al" (اَلْ). In certain particular nouns, the lām of particularization is not pronounced while in others it is pronounced. The rules that govern such assimilations are presented below.

a) LĀM ASH-SHAMSIYYA لَامُ الشَّمْسِيَّةُ

The letter lām of particularization will not be pronounced if followed by any one of the following fourteen letters of the Arabic Alphabet known as "Sun Letters" (اَلْحُرُوفُ الشَّمْسِيَّةُ). These letters assimilate the lām of the article and conditions of complete merger اِدْغَامُ التَّامّ بِلاَ غُنَّة , without nasalization prevail.

1	2	3	4	5	6	7
ط	ث	ص	ر	ت	ض	ذ
طِبْ	ثُمَّ	صِلْ	رَحِمًا	تَفُزْ	ضِفْ	ذَا
8	9	10	11	12	13	14
ن	د	س	ظ	ز	ش	ل
نِعَمْ	دَعْ	سُوءَ	ظَنّ	زُرْ	شَرِيفًا	لِلْكَرَم

EXAMPLES:

ASH-SHAMS اَلشَّمْسُ
AD-DUNYĀ اَلدُّنْيَا
AR-RAHMĀN اَلرَّحْمٰنُ

It is to be noted that the "Sun Letters" are always mushaddad, and a complete Idghām without ghunna is observed with them.

The only exception is the letter nūn where Idghām with ghunna takes place due to nūn mushaddad as discussed in the previous section on Nūn and Mīm Mushaddad. The nasalization of nūn mushaddad should be equal to two ḥaraka.

AN-NĀS اَلنَّاسُ
AN-NĀR اَلنَّارُ

Lām Ta'rif is always sākin (without ḥaraka) and is never followed by the letter Alif. However, there is only one exception to this rule where Lām Ta'rif in the Holy Qur'an has been followed by the letter Alif :

Qur'an 49: بِئْسَ الاِسْمُ (Bisa'l-ismu)

b) LĀM AL-QAMARIYYA اَللاَّمُ الْقَمَرِيَّةُ

The letter lām is pronounced if followed by the remaining fourteen letters of the Arabic Alphabet. These letters are known as "Moon Letters" (اَلْحُرُوفُ الْقَمَرِيَّةُ). They do not assimilate the lām of the definite article.

1	2	3	4	5	6	7
ء	ب	غ	ح	ج	ك	و
8	9	10	11	12	13	14
خ	ف	ع	ق	ي	م	ه

The above fourteen letters are found in: اِبْغِ حَجَّكَ وَخَفْ عَقِيمَهُ

EXAMPLES:

AL-QAMAR اَلْقَمَرُ
AL-KARĪM اَلْكَرِيمُ
AL-QURAISH اَلْقُرَيْشُ

Note that the pronunciation of Lām al-Qamariyya is with Iẓhār, i.e., no nasalization (*ghunna*) or lengthening (*madd*).

THE VERB LĀM لَامُ الْفِعْلِ

The following rules are observed in pronouncing the lām in verbs:

a) The lām is pronounced with Iẓhār if it comes at the beginning or in the middle of a verb. For example:

فِئَتَيْنِ الْتَقَتَا

Lām at the beginning of a verb

قُلْنَا ، جَعَلْنَا

Lām in the middle of a verb

b) The lām is assimilated if followed by a rā or a lām. For example:

PRONOUNCED		WRITTEN	
Bar-rafa'hu	بَرَّفَعَهُ	بَلْ رَفَعَهُ	(lām followed by a rā)
Wa Qul-lahuma	وَقُلَّهُمَا	وَقُلْ لَهُمَا	(lām followed by a lām)

The only exception to the above rules is when there is a sakta between the two words. In this case, no idghām takes place and lām is pronounced with iẓhār. There is only one place in the Holy Qur'an where lām is followed by a rā and a sakta occurs between the two words:

كَلَّا بَلْ ~ رَانَ

Sakta, a pause between two words

(Al-Mutaffifin 83:14)

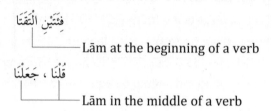

THE RULES OF LETTER MĪM SĀKIN

اَحْكَامُ حَرْفِ الْمِيمِ السَّاكِنَة

THE RULES OF MĪM SĀKIN

The letter mīm is pronounced with both lips and it is known as labial consonant اَلْحَرْفُ الشَّفَوِيَّة . The quality of Iẓhār, Idghām, and lkhfā is also possible in case of sākin mīm under certain conditions. In order to distinguish these qualities of sākin mīm with sākin nūn and tanwīn, the word labial (شَفَوِيٌّ) is prefixed before lzhār, Idghām, and Ikhfā' as follows:

1. Labial Iẓhār اِظْهَارٌ شَفَوِيٌّ
2. Labial Idghām اِدْغَامٌ شَفَوِيٌّ
3. Labial Ikhfā' اِخْفَاءٌ شَفَوِيٌّ

The conditions for Labial Iẓhār, Labial Idghām, and Labial Ikhfā' are two words, the first one ending in mīm sākin and the second word must begin with any letter except bā or mīm for lzhār, mushaddad mīm for Idghām or letter bā for Ikhfā' as explained below.

1. LABIAL IZHĀR OF MĪM SĀKIN اِظْهَارٌ شَفَوِيٌّ

If after mīm sākin, the next word begins with any of the Arabic letters other than letter bā ب and mīm م , then there will be lzhār. The lzhār of mīm sākin is pronounced clearly and sharply without nasalization (ghunna) or prolongation (madd), e.g:

first word ends in mīm sākin

كُنْتُمْ صٰدِقِينَ

second word begins with a letter which is not bā (ب) or mīm (م).

EXAMPLES:

لَكُمْ دِينُكُمْ	لَهُمْ جَنَّتٌ	كُنْتُمْ تَعْلَمُونَ	وَهُمْ فِيهَا

Note that the Iẓhār of mīm sākin requires that once sākin mīm is pronounced by joining both lips, the lips should not remain joining but must be quickly separated to pronounce the next word. If the lips remain in contact, the sound will become nasalized or ghunna and it will be Idghām instead of lzhār of mīm sākin.

2. IDGHĀM OF MĪM SĀKIN اِدْغَامٌ شَفَوِيٌّ

If after mīm sākin, there is a mushaddad mīm (مّ), then there will be Idghām. The merger of mīm sākin into the mushaddad mīm will be with nasalization (ghunna), e.g:

first word ends in mīm sākin

Lahumma لَهُمْ مَا = لَهُمَّا

second word begins with mushaddad mīm

EXAMPLES:

Amman اَمْ مَنْ = اَمَّنْ

Kammin كَمْ مِنْ = كَمِّنْ

3. IKHFĀ OF MĪM SĀKIN اِخْفَاءٌ شَفَوِيٌّ

When the letter bā (ب) comes after mīm sākin, there will be Ikhfā' of mīm sākin. The Ikhfā' is pronounced with a light sound in the nose, half way between Iẓhār (clear) and Idghām (merger), e.g:

first word ends in mīm sākin

رَبُّهُمْ بِهِمْ

second word begins with bā

EXAMPLES:

اَمْ بِهِ

وَهُمْ بِالْاٰخِرَةِ

وَمَاهُمْ بِمُؤْمِنِينَ

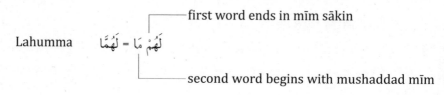

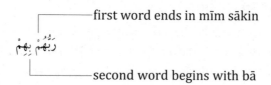

THE RULE OF MUSHADDAD MĪM AND MUSHADDAD NŪN

اَحْكَامُ الْمِيمِ الْمُشَدَّدَةِ وَالنُّونِ الْمُشَدَّدَةِ

THE RULE OF MĪM MUSHADDAD اَحْكَامُ الْمِيمِ الْمُشَدَّدَةِ

The letter mīm with tashdīd (مّ) is always pronounced (whether in continuous recitation اَلْوَصْلُ or stop اَلْوَقْفُ) with nasalization (ghunna). The length of ghunna sound should be equal to two ḥaraka.

EXAMPLES:

مِمَّا	اَللّٰهُمَّ	عَمَّ

THE RULE OF NŪN MUSHADDAD اَحْكَامُ النُّونِ الْمُشَدَّدَةِ

Like mushaddad mīm, mushaddad nūn (نّ) is also pronounced (whether in continuous recitation اَلْوَصْلُ or stop اَلْوَقْفُ with nasalization (ghunna). The length of ghunna sound should be equal to two ḥaraka.

EXAMPLES:

لَتَرَوُنَّ الْجَحِيمَ	جَنَّةٌ	اِنَّ

Note: The mushaddad mīm or mushaddad nūn must be in the same word and it is not a result of merger into mīm or nūn in the next word.

In case of waqf on a mushaddad mīm (مّ) or mushaddad nūn (نّ), the ghunna sound must be a little forceful to indicate the original tashdīd on mīm or nūn.

CHART NO. 4: HEAVY OR THICK PRONUNCIATION OF "RĀ"

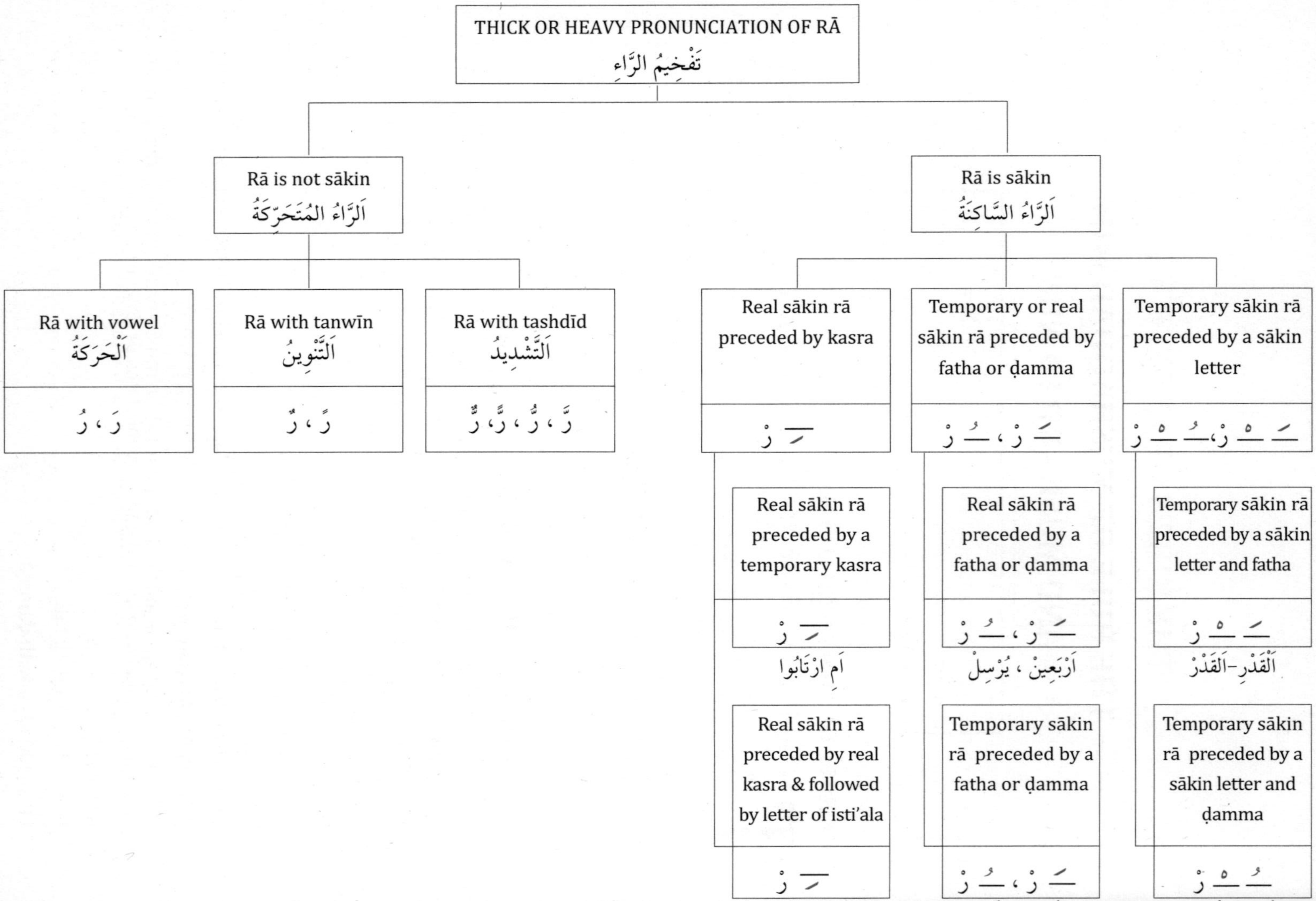

THE RULES OF LETTER RĀ

اَحْكَامُ الْحَرْفِ الرَّاءِ

The letter ر (rā) possesses a quality known as Mukarrarah (مُكَرَّرَةٌ). This quality gives "rā" a vibrating sound. It is articulated with the tip of the tongue rapidly touching the alveolar ridge.

The letter "rā" can be pronounced in one of the two ways depending upon certain conditions. When it is pronounced with a heavy or thick voice, a sort of velarization, it is known as *Tafkhīm of Rā* (تَفْخِيمُ الرَّاءِ). When it is pronounced with a soft or thin voice, without velarization, it is known as *Tarqīq of Rā* (تَرْقِيقُ الرَّاءِ).

The rules that dictate whether to pronounce the letter rā with a 'thick' or 'thin' voice are presented below. A summary of these rules is given in charts No. 4 and 5.

HEAVY OR THICK QUALITY OF RĀ تَفْخِيمُ الرَّاءِ

The letter rā is pronounced with a heavy or thick voice under the following conditions:

1. RĀ IS NOT SĀKIN

a. Rā with ḥaraka (fatha or ḍamma) : رَ ، رُ

Examples:

Rā with fatha اِرَمَ

Rā with ḍamma رُبَمَا

b. Rā with tanwīn (double fatha or double ḍamma): رًا ، رٌ

Examples:

Rā with double fatha مِصْرًا

Rā with double ḍamma نُورٌ

c. Rā Mushaddad (with fatha, ḍamma, double fatha or double ḍamma): رَّ ، رُّ ، رًّا ، رٌّ

Examples:

Mushaddad rā with fatha مَرَّ

Mushaddad rā with ḍamma اَلْبِرُّ

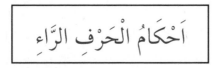

CHART NO. 5: THIN OR LIGHT PRONUNCIATION OF "RĀ"

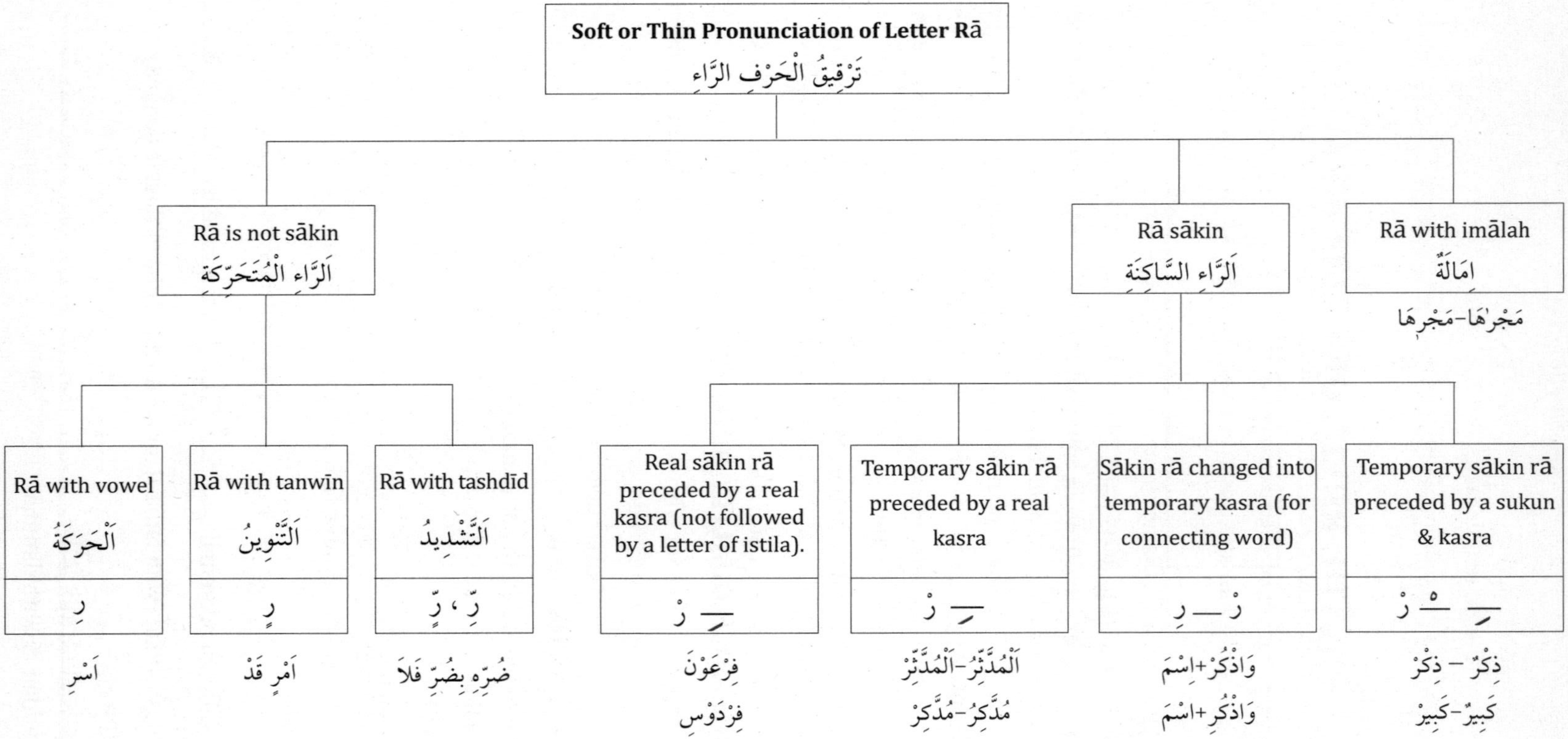

Mushaddad rā with double fatha سِرًّا
Mushaddad rā with double ḍamma ضُرٌّ

2. RĀ IS SĀKIN

a. A sākin rā can have a real sukūn or it can have temporary sukūn due to waqf. The rā will be pronounced with a heavy voice if:

- Rā has a real sukūn and it is preceded by a fatha or ḍamma: ـَ ر ، ـُ ر

Examples:

Real sākin rā with fatha before it اَرْبَعِينَ

Real sākin rā with ḍamma before it يُرْسِلُ

- Rā has a temporary sukūn and it is preceded by a fatha or ḍamma: ـَ ر ، ـُ ر

Examples:

WITH WAQF ON RĀ	WITHOUT WAQF ON RĀ
وَالْقَمَرْ	وَالْقَمَرِ
بِالنُّذُرْ	بِالنُّذُرِ

b. Temporary sākin rā preceded by a real sākin letter (except ى) which is preceded by a fatha or ḍamma: ـَ ـْ ر ، ـُ ـْ ر

Examples:

Temporary sākin rā preceded by a sākin letter and fatha اَلْقَدْرِ – اَلْقَدْرْ

Temporary sākin rā preceded by a sākin letter and ḍamma اَلْعُسْرِ – اَلْعُسْرْ

c. A real sākin rā can have a temporary Kasra or a real Kasra. The rā will be pronounced with a voice if:

- Real sākin rā preceded by a temporary Kasra: ـِ ر

Example:

اَمْ + اِرْتَابُوا – اَمِ ارْتَابُوا

Temporary Kasra used to connect اَمْ with اِرْتَابُوا

- Real sākin rā preceded by a real Kasra and followed by a letter of Isti'la.[33]

ـِ ر + حَرْفُ الْاِسْتِعْلَاءِ

[33] The letters of Isti'la are: خ ، ص ، ض ، ط ، ظ ، غ ، ق

They are pronounced with an elevated voice. The rā will be pronounced with heavy voice تَفْخِيمُ الرَّاءِ if it is followed by a letter of isti'la as mentioned before.

Examples:

قِرْطَاس	مِرْصَادْ

SOFT OR THIN QUALITY OF RĀ (تَرْقِيقُ الرَّاءِ)

The letter rā is pronounced with a soft or thin voice under the following conditions:

1. RĀ IS NOT SĀKIN

a. Rā with Kasra:

Example: اَسْرِ

b. Rā with double Kasra: رٍ

Example: اَمْرٍ قَدْ

c. Rā with Tashdīd and Kasra or double Kasra: رِّ ، رٍّ

Examples:

Mushaddad rā with Kasra ضُرِّهٖ

Mushaddad rā with double Kasra بِضُرٍّ فَلَا

2. RĀ IS SĀKIN

a. The letter rā can have a real sukūn on it or a temporary sukūn due to waqf. When rā is sākin, it will be pronounced softly under the following conditions:

- Real sākin rā preceded by a Kasra provided that a letter of Isti'la does not follow rā sākin: * رْ ـِـ

  * No letter of Isti'la follows

  Example: فِرْدَوْس
- Temporary sākin rā preceded by a real Kasra: ـِـ

  Examples: اَلْمُدَّثِّرِ – اَلْمُدَّثِّرْ

  مُدَّكِرِ – مُدَّكِرْ

b. Real sākin rā is replaced by a temporary Kasra for connecting two words:

* + رْ ـِـ

* a word beginning with hamza

Example:

وَاذْكُرِ اسْمَ ——— وَاذْكُرْ + اِسْمَ

temporary kasra — Real sākin rā

c. Temporary sākin rā preceded by a sākin letter (except ي) which has a real Kasra before it[34]: ـِـ ـْـ رْ

Example:

ذِكْرٌ – ذِكْرْ

سِحْرٌ – سِحْرْ

d. Temporary sākin rā preceded by a sākin yā which has a real Kasra or fatha before it: ـَـ يْ رْ ، ـِـ يْ رْ

Example:

كَبِيرٌ – كَبِيرْ

خَيْرٌ – خَيْرْ

3. RĀ WITH IMĀLA

The letter rā is also pronounced softly in case of Imāla (اِمَالَةٌ). Imāla means the inclination of letter alif towards the letter yā in such a way that the sound is between alif and yā. There is only one place in the Holy Qur'an where Imām Hafs (اِمَامْ حَفْصْ) has used Imāla and pronounced the rā softly.

PRONOUNCED AS	WRITTEN AS
مَجْرٖهَا	مَجْرٰهَا
MAJ-RIY-HĀ	MAJ-RĀ -HĀ

[34] Two sākin letters cannot occur together except in case of waqf (stopping), for example: in the word ذِكْرٌ (dhikrun), kāf is sākin (كْ) and rā has tanwīn (رٌ) but when waqf is made, then the last letter of the word become sākin ذِكْرْ (dhikr).

THE RULES OF ASSIMILATION

اَحْكَامُ الْاِدْغَامِ الْمُتَمَاثِلَيْنِ وَالْاِدْغَامِ
الْمُتَجَانِسَيْنِ وَالْاِدْغَامُ الْمُتَقَارِبَيْنِ

In the Rules of Nūn sakīn and Tanwīn, we covered assimilation or merger of Nūn sakīn or Tanwīn with or without nasalization. In this section, the rules of assimilation of letters other than Nūn sakīn or Tanwīn are presented.

CONDITIONS FOR MERGER

The following conditions are required for merger:

(a) Two letters must occur together, either in the same word or in two consecutive words.

(b) First letter must be sākin.

(c) Second letter must be mutaḥarrik with tashdīd.

(d) Two letters must be from one of the following three categories:

1. Two identical letters
   (Same place of articulation مَخْرَجٌ and same quality صِفَةٌ)
2. Two letters of the same place of articulation مَخْرَجٌ but different quality صِفَاتٌ.
3. Two letters of the close places of articulation.

1. MERGER OF TWO IDENTICAL LETTERS اِدْغَامُ الْمُتَمَاثِلَيْنِ

When two identical letters occur together, then the first one is completely merged into the second one without nasalization:

PRONOUNCED WRITTEN

قَدَّخَلُوا = قَدْ دَخَلُوا

- two identical letters (د)
- first letter is sākin (دْ)
- second letter is mutaharrik with tashdīd (دَّ)

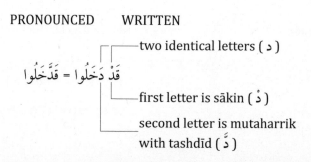

EXAMPLES:

IDENTICAL LETTERS		PRONOUNCED	WRITTEN
Bā ب	into Bā ب	اِضْرِبّعَصَاكَ	اِضْرِبْ بِعَصَاكَ
Tā ت	into Tā ت	فَمَا رَبِحَتّجَارَتُهُمْ	فَمَا رَبِحَتْ تِجَارَتُهُمْ
Rā ر	into Rā ر	وَاذْكُرَّبَّكَ	وَاذْكُرْ رَبَّكَ
Dhāl ذ	into Dhāl ذ	اِذَّهَبَ	اِذْ ذَهَبَ
‘Ain ع	into ‘Ain ع	تَسْتَطِعَّلَيْهِ	تَسْتَطِعْ عَلَيْهِ
Lām ل	into Lām ل	بَلاَّيَخَافُونَ	بَلْ لَايَخَافُونَ

EXCEPTIONS

There will be no merger of two identical letters under the following conditions:

(a) If both identical letters are mutaḥarrik (voweled), then both must be pronounced:

two identical letters (ب)

ذَهَبَ بِسَمْعِهِمْ

first letter is mutaḥarrik (بَ)

second letter is mutaḥarrik (بِ)

two identical letters (ع)

يَشْفَعُ عِنْدَهُ

first letter is mutaḥarrik (عُ)

second letter is mutaḥarrik (عِ)

(b) If both letters are letter of Madd either waw or yā then there will be no merger:

Letter of Madd waw:

two identical letters of Madd (و)

هَادُوا وَالنَّصَارَى

first letter is sākin (وْ)

second letter is mutaḥarrik (وَ)

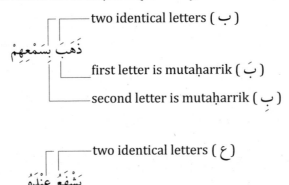

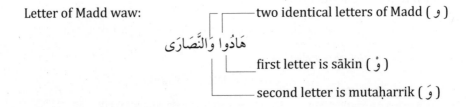

Letter of Madd yā:

فِي يَوْمٍ

two identical letters of Madd (ي)

first letter is sākin (يْ)

second letter is mutaḥarrik (يَ)

Note: In case the letters of Madd are Līn letters (waw or yā preceded by fatha) then there will be a complete merger without nasalization.

Example:

PRONOUNCED		WRITTEN
بِمَا عَصَوَّكَانُوا	—	بِمَا عَصَوْا وَكَانُوا
Complete merger of waw without nasalisation		fatha before the letter of madd

(c) If there is a Sakta between the two identical letters, then there will be no merger:

(al-Haqqa 28) مَالِيَهْ ۜ هَلَكَ

Sakta between two words

two identical letters

2. MERGER OF TWO LETTERS OF THE SAME PLACE OF ARTICULATION اِدْغَامُ الْمُتَجَانِسَيْنِ

When two letters, having the same place of articulation مَخْرَجٌ but different qualities صِفَاتٌ, occur together, then the first one is merged completely into the second without nasalization.

(a) MERGER OF DENTAL CONSONANTS Tā ت , Dāl د and Ṭā ط

The Dental Consonants have the same point of articulation (makhraj); they are pronounced with the tip of the tongue against the roots of the upper incisors teeth. However, they have different qualities.

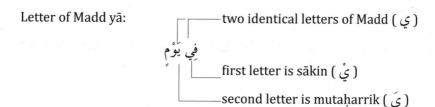

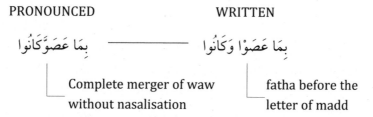

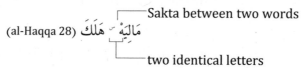

MERGER OF DĀL د INTO TĀ ت :

(al-Baqarah 2:28) قَدْ تَبَيَّنَ = قَتَّبَيَّنَ

- two letters dāl د and tā ت have the same Makhraj but different qualities
- first letter is sākin (دْ)
- second letter is mutaḥarrik (تَ)

MERGER OF TĀ ت INTO ṬĀ ط :

(Al 'Imrān 4:122) هَمَّتْ طَآئِفَةٌ = هَمَّطَّآئِفَةٌ

- two letters tā ت and ṭā ط have the same Makhraj but different qualities
- first letter is sākin (تُ)
- second letter is mutaḥarrik (طَّ)

MERGER OF TĀ ت INTO DAL د :

(Al-A'rāf 7:189) اَثْقَلَتْ دَعَوْا = اَثْقَلَدَّعَوْا

- two letters tā ت and dāl د have the same Makhraj but different qualities
- first letter is sākin (تْ)
- second letter is mutaḥarrik (دَّ)

(b) MERGER OF ALVEO-DENTAL CONSONANTS thā ث , dhāl ذ , and ẓā ظ

The Alveo-dental consonants have the same point of articultion (makhraj): the tip of the tongue touch the edges of upper front teeth, but their qualities are different.

MERGER OF DHĀL ذ INTO ẒĀ ظ :

(az-Zukhrūf 39) اِذْ ظَلَمْتُمْ= اِظَّلَمْتُمْ

- two letters dhāl ذ and ẓā ظ have the same Makhraj but different qualities
- first letter is sākin (ذْ)
- second letter is mutaḥarrik (ظَ)

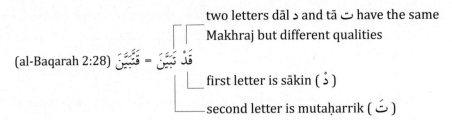

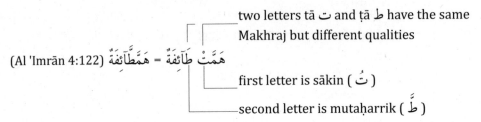

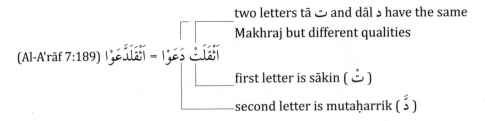

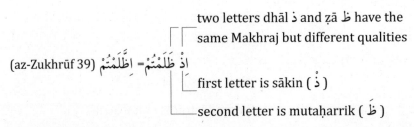

MERGER OF THĀ ث INTO DHĀL ذ :

(Al-A'rāf 7:176) يَلْهَذّٰلِكَ = يَلْهَثْ ذٰلِكَ

The letters of thā ث and dhāl ذ have the same Makhraj but different qualities

first letter is sākin (ثْ)

second letter is mutaḥarrik (ذَ)

(c) MERGER OF LABIAL CONSONANTS bā ب and mīm م

The Labial Consonants have the same point of articulation (makhraj): they are pronounced with the lips but the quality with which they are pronounced differs.

(Hud 42) ارْكَمَّعَنَا = ارْكَبْ مَعَنَا

two letters bā ب and mim م have the same Makhraj but different qualities

first letter is sākin (بْ)

second letter is mutaḥarrik (مَ)

3. MERGER OF TWO LETTERS OF CLOSE PLACES OF ARTICULATION اِدْغَامُ الْمُتَقَارِبَيْنِ

When two letters having a close place of articulation (makhraj) occur together, the first one is completely merged into the second without nasalization.

MERGER OF ALVEOLAR CONSONANTS lām ل , rā ر , and nūn ن

The Alveolar consonants are articulated from very close makhraj مَخْرَجٌ with different qualities (refer to chapter 3 for detail). The merger of nūn sakīn and tanwīn was covered earlier in this chapter.

MERGER OF LĀM ل INTO RĀ ر :

PRONOUNCED WRITTEN

(Al-Isrā' 24) قُرَّبِّ = قُلْ رَبِّ

The letters of lām ل and rā ر are of two close makhārij مَخَارِجٌ

first letter is sākin (لْ)

second letter is mutaḥarrik (رَ)

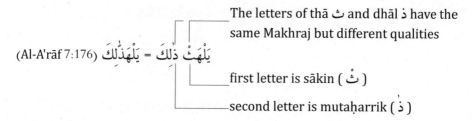

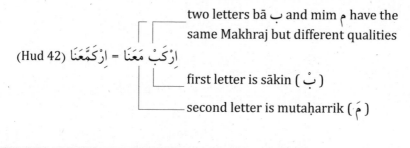

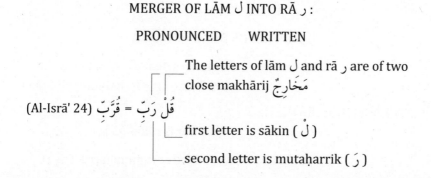

MERGER OF Ṭā ط INTO Tā ت :

PRONOUNCED WRITTEN

two letters ṭā ط and tā ت are of two close makhārij مَخَارِجٌ

(al-Maedah 5:28) لَئِنْ بَسَطْتَ=لَئِنْ بَسَتَّ

first letter is sākin (طْ)

second letter is mutaḥarrik (تَ)

MERGER OF Qāf ق INTO Kāf ك :

PRONOUNCED WRITTEN

two letters qāf ق and kāf ك are of two close makhārij مَخَارِجٌ

(al-Mursalat 77) اَلَمْ نَخْلُقْكُمْ= اَلَمْ نَخْلُكُّمْ

first letter is sākin (قْ)

second letter is mutaḥarrik (كُ)

EXCEPTIONS

There will be no merger of two close makhārij letters if:
there is a sakta between the two letters:

Sakta between

(al-Mutaffifin14) كَلَّا بَلْ رَانَ

two close makhārij letters

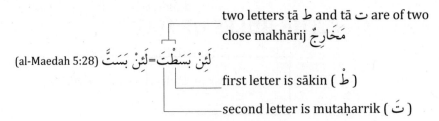

THE RULES OF MADD

اَحْكَامُ الْمَدِّ

Madd مَدّ means to exaggerate the lengthening of sound in the pronunciation of the letters alif ا , waw و , and yā ي , when sākin under certain conditions. These three sākin letters (ا ، و ، ي) are known as the letters of Madd (اَلْحُرُوفُ الْمَدّ) since Madd or lengthening never occurs on any other letter.

The lengthening of the letters of Madd in pronunciation is measured in terms of the number of ḥarakāt. One ḥaraka is equal to the time required to pronounce a fatha (ـَ = a), a ḍamma (ـُ = u) or a kasra (ـِ = i). Some people measure the lengthening in terms of "the duration of number of alifs." One alif is equal to two ḥarakat. Thus two alifs are equal to four ḥarakat, three alifs are equal to six ḥarakat, and so on. To avoid any confusion between the alif letter and the "duration of alif," we will use the number of ḥarakat rather than alifs to indicate the lengthening of the letters of Madd.

The lengthening of the letters of Madd can be short قَصْرٌ (two ḥarakāt), average تَوَسُّط (four ḥarakāt) or long طُول (six ḥarakāt).

HAMZA AND ALIF

The letter alif is always sākin in Arabic (no vowel or ḥaraka) as mentioned in Chapter Two. If there is a sign of a vowel (fatha, ḍamma, or kasra) on it, it is called hamza (ء). Alif is always preceded by a letter with fatha which lengthens the pronunciation of the fatha to two times.

For example:

Mā مَا (where ā = aa, a long vowel)

Lā لَا

The reader is cautioned here that in the copies of the Holy Qur'an printed in Middle Eastern countries (known as the 'Uthmanic text' الرَّسْمُ الْخَطِّ الْعُثْمَانِي) alif is given ḥaraka with a hamza on it as follows: أَ ، أُ ، إِ

Whereas in some countries, including Turkey, India, Pakistan, and Bangladesh, it is written without hamza: اَ ، اُ ، اِ

In either case, it should be remembered that there is a hamza when alif is mutaḥarrik (voweled). When hamza occurs in a word or at the end of a word, it is always written as head of letter 'ain (ء) in 'Uthmanic as well as non-'Uthmanic texts of the Holy Qur'an.

The reader is further advised to review the terms and definitions presented in Table 5. These terms will be used in the discussion of Madd.

REQUIREMENTS OF MADD

The following conditions are necessary for Madd to occur:

1. A letter of Madd (known as a Condition of Madd (اَلشَّرْطُ الْمَدِّ) must be present in a word.
2. A hamza, sukūn, or shadda (known as a Cause of Madd (اَلسَّبَبُ الْمَدِّ) must immediately follow a letter of Madd.
3. The letter of Madd must be used in pronunciation (if it is dropped in continuous recitation اَلْوَصْل, no Madd occurs).

TYPES OF MADD اَقْسَامُ الْمَدِّ

There are two types of Madd as follows:

1. PRIMARY OR NATURAL MADD اَلْمَدُّ الْأَصْلِيُّ اَوِ الْمَدُّ الطَّبِيعِيُّ
2. SECONDARY OR DERIVED MADD اَلْمَدُّ الْفَرْعِيُّ

1. PRIMARY OR NATURAL MADD الْمَدُّ الْاَصْلِيُّ اَوِ الْمَدُّ الطَّبِيعِيُّ

When the letters of Madd (alif, waw, yā) are preceded by a ḥaraka and not followed by a real or temporary sākin letter, a hamza, or a mushaddad letter then the Primary or Natural Madd is formed. The prolongation of the Natural Madd is equal to two ḥaraka. The first ḥaraka is due to the preceding letter and the second is due to letters of Madd: alif, waw, or yā. If a word is not pronounced with a Natural Madd, then it becomes a different word. For example:

Inna اِنَّ (Indeed): there is a fatha on nūn but no Madd.

Inna اِنَّا (Indeed, we): there is a fatha followed by a letter of Madd (alif); therefore, it must be prolonged to two ḥaraka.

The explanation and examples of Natural Madd formed due to alif, waw, and yā are given in the following pages.

TABLE 5: SUMMARY OF TERMS AND DEFINITIONS

NO.	ARABIC WORDS	MEANING / EXPLANATION	EXAMPLES
1.	ḤARAKA اَلْحَرَكَة	A vowel mark: fatha (ـَ), ḍamma (ـُ), or kasra (ـِ)	صَدَقَ يُوسُفُ فِيهِ
2.	MUTAḤARRIK اَلْمُتَحَرِّك	A letter with a vowel (ḥaraka)	حَيْثُ
3.	SUKŪN اَلسُّكُون	Absence of a vowel mark or ḥaraka (ـْ)	مِنْ ، كُنْ
4.	REAL SUKŪN اَلسُّكُونُ الْاَصْلِيُّ	A real sukūn is part of a letter in a word and is always pronounced in continuous recitation or stopping.	فِرْعَوْنُ قُلْنَا جَعَلْنَا
5.	TEMPORARY SUKŪN اَلسُّكُونُ الْعَارِض	This sukūn is due to waqf on a word.	وَالْقَمَرَ – وَالْقَمَرْ
6.	WAṢL اَلْوَصْل	This is continuous recitation without stopping or breaking the breath.	
7.	WAQF اَلْوَقْف	It means to stop recitation; recitation is resumed with a new breath.	نَسْتَعِينُ – نَسْتَعِينْ اَلْمَغْفِرَةُ – اَلْمَغْفِرَةْ
8.	HAMZATU'L-WAṢL هَمْزَةُ الْوَصْلِ	This is a hamza in the beginning of certain verbs and nouns. It is always pronounced as a single word. However, in continuous reading (اَلْوَصْل) it is dropped (not pronounced).	اَمْ+اِرْتَابُوا اَمِ ارْتَابُوا hamzatu'l-wasl
9.	REAL KASRA اَلْكَسْرَةُ الْاَصْلِيُّ	It is a kasra which cannot be separated from the letter. It is always pronounced.	فِرْعَوْنُ
10.	TEMPORARY KASRA اَلْكَسْرَةُ الْعَارِض	In certain words when read together, the last letter in the first word is given a kasra to connect it with the second word; the hamza at the beginning of the second word is not pronounced.	اَمْ+اِرْتَابُوا اَمِ ارْتَابُوا temporary kasra
11.	TASHDĪD اَلتَّشْدِيدُ	When a letter occurs twice without a vowel (ḥaraka) between them, it is written only once and a sign called tashdīd (ـّ) is placed over it.	كُلِّ اُمَّةٌ جَنَّةٌ

12.	SHADDA اَلشَّدَّةُ	The sign of tashdīd (ّ) is known as shadda.	مُحَمَّدٌ
13.	MUSHADDAD اَلْمُشَدَّدُ	A letter with tashdīd is called mushaddad. This letter must be pronounced twice: first as sākin (connecting by the previous ḥaraka) and then with ḥaraka.	كُلّ = كُلْل أُمُّهُ = أُمْمُهُ جَنَّةٌ = جَنْنَةٌ
14.	MUKHAFFAF اَلْمُخَفَّفُ	A sākin letter is also known as *mukhaffaf.*	See Sukūn
15.	MUTHAQQAL اَلْمُثَقَّلُ	A letter with tashdīd is also known as *muthaqqal.*	See Mushaddad
16.	KALĪMĪ كَلِمِيٌّ	It refers to a word.	قُرْآنٌ ، مُحَمَّدٌ ، صَدَقَ
17.	HARFĪ حَرْفِيٌّ	It refers to a letter.	م ، ن ، ط ،...
18.	LĪN LETTER اَلْحَرْفُ اللِّينُ	The letter waw and yā when preceded by a fatha are known as Waw Līn and Yā Līn respectively. Līn letters are always pronounced softly.	خَوْفَ حَيْثُ
19.	MUQATTA'ĀT اَلْمُقَطَّعَاتُ	A number of sūras are prefixed with abbreviated letters. They are written together as a word but pronounced as separate letters. (The name of a letter when pronounced becomes a "word"; the letter س is pronounced as سين which consists of three letters (س ي ن). In the rules of Madd, the pronunciation format is used to determine if there is a condition of Madd (alif, waw, or yā) and a cause of Madd (hamza, sukūn, or tashdīd) in the abbreviated letters.	الٓمٓ – اَلِفْ لَامْ مِيمْ طٰهٰ – طَاهَا يٰسٓ – يَاسِينْ صٓ – صَادْ

a. ALIF MADD اَلِفْ مَدّ

Alif Madd is always sākin and is preceded by a fatha (ا ـَ). It is pronounced by doubling the sound of fatha (two ḥaraka).

Example:

fatha on the letter qāf

Qāla قَالَ

condition of Madd (alif)

(ā = aa = two fatha) next letter is mutaḥarrik (no hamza, sukūn or shadda)

The usual way of writing an alif is as in the above example of قَالَ, but in some words it is denoted by a small line over the letter known as vertical Alif also known as Alif Maqsūra:

dhāl ذ is considered to have a fatha

Dhālika ذٰلِكَ = ذَالِكَ

condition of Madd (alif) written as Alif Maqsūra

Next letter is Mutaḥarrik (no hamza, sukūn or shadda)

b. WAW MADD وَاوْ مَدّ

Like Alif Madd, Waw Madd is also sākin but it is preceded by a ḍamma (و ـُ). It is pronounced by prolonging the sound of ḍamma (two ḥaraka).

Example:

damma on the letter qāf

Yunfiqūna يُنْفِقُونَ

condition of Madd (waw)

(ū = uu = two damma) the next letter is mutaḥarrik (no hamza, sukūn or shadda)

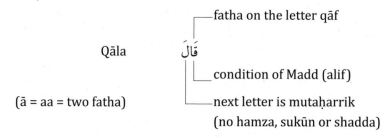

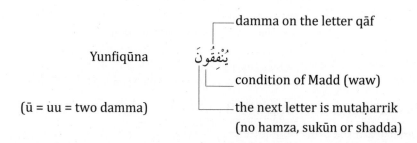

If sākin waw is preceded by a fatha (و ـَـ) and followed by a ḥaraka, it is known as soft waw وَاوٌ لَيِّنَةٌ which is pronounced softly without lengthening the sound of waw:

Waw Līn (soft waw): سَوْفَ
- the letter with fatha
- condition of Madd (waw sākin)
- next letter is mutaḥarrik (no hamza, sukūn or shadda)

But if the letter of Madd is followed by a sākin letter, it is not a Waw Madd. In this case, it is known as Madd 'Āriḍ اَلْمَدُّ الْعَارِضُ (a type of Derived Madd) which will be covered later in this chapter.

Madd 'Āriḍ خَوْفْ
- letter khā with fatha
- condition of Madd (waw sākin)
- next letter after letter of Madd is sākin (cause of Madd)

c. YĀ MADD يَاءُ مَدٍّ

If the letter before yā sākin is a kasra (ي ـِـ) and yā sākin is followed by a ḥaraka, it is called Yā Madd:

Example:

Yurīdu = يُرِيدُ
- the letter rā with kasra
- condition of Madd (yā sākin)
- next letter is mutaḥarrik (no hamza, sukūn or shadda)

In some words, yā is not written in the usual way, instead a small vertical line is placed underneath the preceding letter:

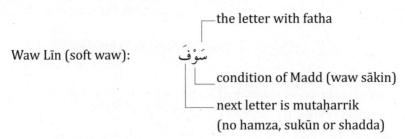

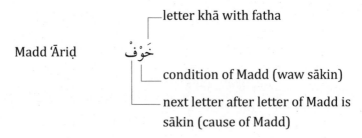

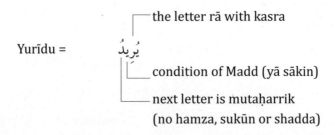

letter hā with kasra

Ibrahīm = اِبْرَاهِيم = اِبْرٰهِيم

condition of Madd (yā) written as a vertical line under the letter

next letter is Mutaḥarrik (no hamza, sukūn or shadda)

As in the case of Waw Madd, if the sākin yā is preceded by a fatha (ـَي) instead of kasra, it is known as soft yā يَاءٌ لَيِّنَةٌ which is pronounced softly without any lengthening:

letter hā with fatha

Yā līn (soft yā); حَيْثُ

condition of Madd (yā sākin)

mutaḥarrik letter (no hamza, sukūn or shadda)

Please note that if the Yā Madd is followed by a sākin letter, it is not a Yā Madd. In this case, it is known as Madd 'Āriḍ اَلْمَدُّ الْعَارِضُ (a type of derived Madd) which will be covered later in this chapter.

letter bā with fatha

Madd 'Āriḍ اَلْبَيْتُ

condition of Madd (yā sākin)

next letter after letter of Madd is sākin (cause of Madd)

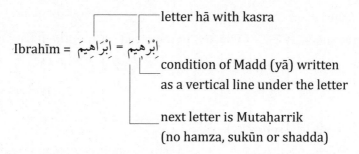

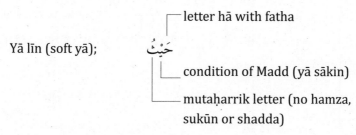

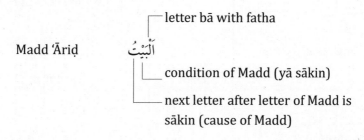

CHART NO. 6: THE RULES OF MADD

Notes:

1. There is no hamza after Talaffuzi form (ـٓهٰ ، ـٰهٰ) If there is a hamza, it is called Elongated Madd (a form of Derived Madd).
2. "2-letters" Abbreviated letters are : ح ى ط ه ر = حى طهر
3. "3-letters" Abbreviated letters are : ن ق ص ع س ل ك م = نقص عسلكم

2/4/6 (triangles): Indicates lengthening of the letter of Madd equal to 2, 4, or 6 harakat are all acceptable

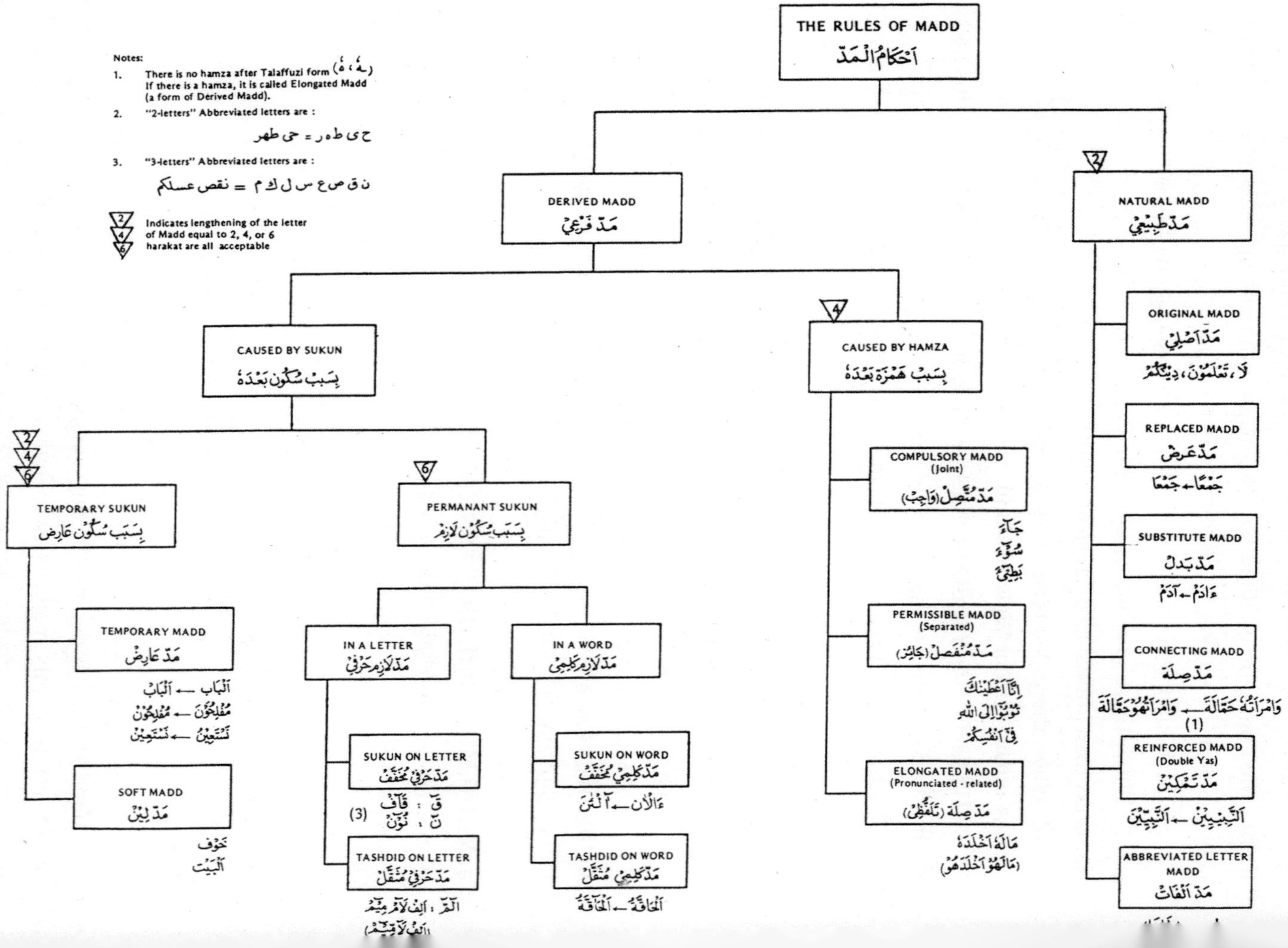

2. SECONDARY OR DERIVED MADD اَلْمَدُّ الْفَرْعِيُّ

If after the Condition of Madd (i.e., the madd letters of alif, waw and yā), there is a hamza, sukūn, or shadda, it is known as Derived Madd.

So the Madd Far'i (secondary madd) is derived from Natural Madd in three ways:

1. When there is a hamza after the Condition of Madd (Alif, waw, or yā), this Hamza is then known as a Cause of Madd.

2. When there is a temporary or real sukūn after the Condition of Madd; this sukūn is then called a Cause of Madd.

3. When there is a Mushaddad letter after the Condition of Madd,[35] the sukūn in the mushaddad letter is the Cause of Madd.

There are five types of Madd Fara'i (Secondary Madd), as explained in the following sections:

TYPES OF SECONDARY MADD

a. Madd Muttaṣil or Wājib	اَلْمَدُّ الْمُتَّصِلُ	(Joint or Compulsory Madd)
b. Madd Munfaṣil or Jāiz	اَلْمَدُّ الْمُنْفَصِلُ	(Separated or Permissible Madd)
c. Madd Ṣilah or Talaffuẓī	اَلْمَدُّ الصِّلَةُ	(Elongated or Pronunciation Related Madd)
d. Madd Lāzim	اَلْمَدُّ اللاَّزِمُ	(Permanent Madd)
e. Madd 'Ariḍ	اَلْمَدُّ الْعَارِضُ	(Temporary Madd)

a. MADD MUTTAṢIL OR WĀJIB اَلْمَدُّ الْمُتَّصِلُ اَوِ الْوَاجِبُ

If after the letter of Madd, there appears a hamza in the same word, it is known as Madd Muttaṣil (Joint Madd).

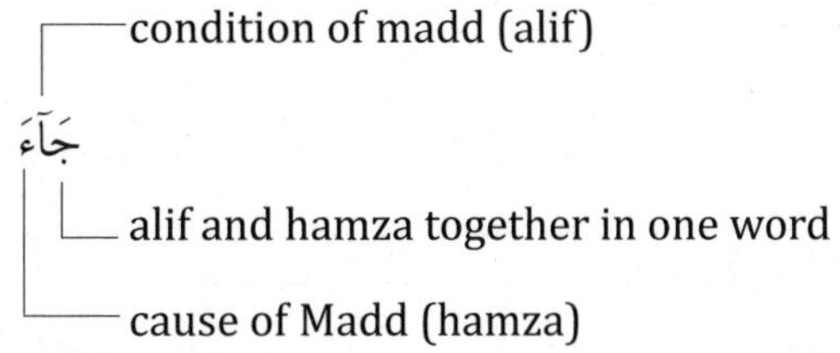

Madd Muttaṣil is denoted by the symbol (~) placed over the letter of madd. The prolongation of this madd is two, four, or five ḥarakāt (short, medium, or long respectively). This madd is also known as Madd Wājib (Compulsory Madd).

---

[35] Recall that mushaddad letter is pronounced twice, first sākin then with ḥaraka. Although the cause of Madd is sukūn, for simplicity, it is treated separately.

EXAMPLES:

Symbol of Madd Muttaṣil (~)

اُولٰٓئِكَ	hamza (Cause of Madd) after alif Maqsūra (Condition of Madd).
سُوْٓءَ	hamza (Cause of Madd) after waw (Condition of Madd)
سِيْٓئَتْ	hamza (Cause of Madd) after yā (Condition of Madd)

b. MADD MUNFAṢIL OR JĀ'IZ اَلْمَدُّ الْمُنْفَصِلُ اَوِ الْجَائِزُ

If the letter of Madd is at the end of a word and the next word begins with hamza, it is called Madd Munfaṣil (Separated Madd):

Symbol of Madd Munfaṣil (~) بِمَآ اُنْزِلَ

- Letter of Madd Alif (Condition of Madd) at the end of the word
- Alif and hamza in two words
- hamza (written as اُ) at the beginning of the second word

Madd Munfaṣil is denoted by the symbol (~) placed over the letter of Madd. The prolongation of this madd is four ḥaraka. This madd is also known as Madd Jā'iz (Permissible Madd).

EXAMPLES:

رَبِّيْٓ اَكْرَمَنْ   قَالُوْٓا اٰمَنَّا   اِنَّآ اَعْطَيْنَا

- first word ending with the letter of Madd (alif, waw, yā)
- second word begins with a hamza, written as (ا or ا)

c. MADD ṢILAH OR TALAFFUẒĪ اَلْمَدُّ الصِّلَةُ اَوِ التَّلَفُّظِيُّ

In some words, the letter of madd waw and yā are not written in the usual way as و or ي . Instead, a vertical line is placed over the preceding letter for waw or a vertical line is placed under the letter for yā as follows:

USUAL FORM		ALTERNATE FORM
هُو	=	هٗ
هِي	=	هٖ

The alternate forms are pronounced like usual waw and yā in the recitation.

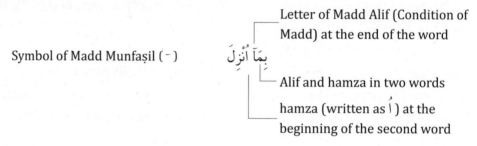

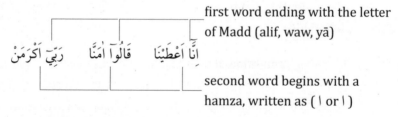

If a hamza follows the alternate form of waw or yā, then Madd Munfaṣil is given different name: Madd Ṣilah or Talaffuẓī (Elongated as Pronunciation Related Madd):

PRONOUNCED AS		WRITTEN AS	
عِنْدَهُوٓ اِلَّا	=	عِنْدَهٗٓ اِلَّا	Alternate form of the letter waw (inverted comma: Condition of Madd); Hamza follows the letter Madd (Cause of Madd)
بِهِيٓ اَنْجَيْنَا	=	بِهٖٓ اَنْجَيْنَا	Alternate form of the letter yā (vertical line: Condition of Madd); Hamza follows the letter of Madd (Cause of Madd)

Note: If the Cause of Madd, hamza, is waṣli that is this hamza is dropped in continuous reading (اَلْوَصْلُ), there will be no madd since the hamza (cause of Madd) is not there:

PRONOUNCED AS		WRITTEN AS	
فِلْ اَرْضِ	=	فِي الْاَرْضِ	hamzatu'l-waṣl (not pronounced), therefore no madd

d. MADD LĀZIM اَلْمَدُّ اللَّازِمُ

If after the letter of Madd, there appears such a sukūn which cannot be separated from the word, Madd Lāzim occurs. Remember that this sukūn is not due to waqf; it is either a real sukūn or the one in the mushaddad letter. A mushaddad letter is always pronounced twice; first with sukūn and then with a vowel (fatha, ḍamma, or kasra).

Note: The letter of Madd and the real sukūn must occur together in the same word for Madd Lāzim. (No Madd Lāzim if two words are involved).

Madd Lāzim can occur in an abbreviated letter (حَرْفِيٌّ) or in a word (كَلِمِيٌّ). Furthermore, it can be caused by a real sukūn or by a mushaddad letter.

Thus, there are four types of Madd Lāzim as follows:

(i) Madd Lāzim Kalimī Mukhaffaf (due to sukūn in a word)

(ii) Madd Lāzim Kalimī Muthaqqal (due to tashdīd in a word)

(iii) Madd Lāzim Harfī Mukhaffaf (due to sukūn in a letter)

(iv) Madd Lāzim Harfī Muthaqqal (due to tashdīd in a letter)

(i) MADD KALIMĪ MUKHAFFAF اَلْمَدُّ الْمُخَفَّفُ الْكَلِمِيُّ

This type of Madd Lāzim is formed due to permanent or real sukūn in a word:

ءَاۤلْئٰنَ = ءَالْاٰنَ
- Condition of Madd (alif)
- one word
- Cause of Madd (Sukūn on lām)

(ii) MADD KALIMĪ MUTHAQQAL اَلْمَدُّ الْمُثَقَّلُ الْكَلِمِيُّ

This is a type of Madd Lāzim in which after the condition of Madd (also known as letter of Madd), there is a mushaddad letter in the same word:

تَحَآضُّونَ
- Condition of Madd (alif)
- one word
- Cause of Madd (Mushaddad letter)

(iii) MADD HARFĪ MUKHAFFAF اَلْمَدُّ الْمُخَفَّفُ الْحَرْفِيُّ

This type of Madd Lāzim is found in the Abbreviated Letters (اَلْحُرُوفُ الْمُقَطَّعَاتُ). The abbreviated letter must be a "three letter" word and must contain the Condition of Madd (alif, waw, or yā) as well as the Cause of Madd (real sukūn). The abbreviated letter ṣād ص is pronounced as صَادْ which consists of three letters: ṣād-alif-dāl.

PRONOUNCED AS WRITTEN AS

Ṣād: صَآدْ = صٓ
- Condition of Madd (alif)
- Abbreviated letter (contains three letters when pronounced: صَاد)
- Cause of Madd (real sukūn)

EXAMPLES:

Qāf: قَآفْ = قٓ
- Condition of Madd (alif)
- Cause of Madd (real sukūn on fā)

Nūn: نُوٓنْ = نٓ
- Condition of Madd (waw)
- Cause of Madd (real sukūn on nūn)

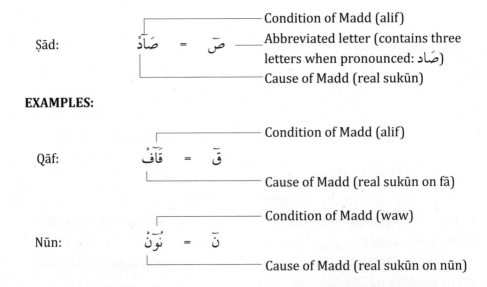

Note: There will be no Madd Harfī Mukhaffaf, if the abbreviated letter does not contain the condition of Madd. The letter Alif is a "three letter" word but there is no condition of Madd in it, hence no Madd:

Alif: ا = اَلِفْ

the letter lām (not a Condition of Madd)

the real sākin letter (Cause of Madd)

(iv) MADD HARFĪ MUTHAQQAL اَلْمَدُّ الْمُثَقَّلُ الْحَرْفِيُّ

This type of Madd Lāzim is found in Abbreviated Letters when there is a tashdīd on them due to assimilation (اِدْغَامٌ) of one letter into another. The Abbreviated Letter must be a "three letter" word and contains a tashdīd:

mushaddad mīm

الٓمّٓ = اَلِفْ لَامْ مِيمْ = اَلِفْ لَامِّيمْ

Due to Labial Idghām, this mīm is merged into mīm of the next letter resulting into mushaddad mīm.

the Condition of Madd (alif)

the Cause of Madd (mushaddad mīm). Mīm is a three letter word: م = مِيم = م ي م

e. MADD 'ĀRIḌ اَلْمَدُّ الْعَارِضُ

If after the letter of Madd, there is a temporary sukūn due to stop (اَلْوَقْفُ) on the word, it is known as Madd 'Āriḍ, or Temporary Madd:

STOPPING

Condition of Madd (waw)

مُفْلِحُونْ

Cause of Madd (temporary Sukūn due to waqf)

TEMPORARY MADD DUE TO WAQF ON NŪN (Muflihūn)

CONTINUOUS RECITATION

Condition of Madd (waw)

مُفْلِحُونَ

no Cause of Madd (hamza, sukūn or shadda)

NO MADD in Muflihūna

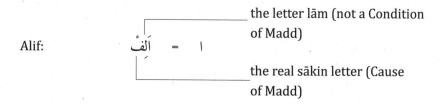

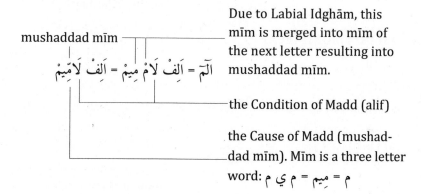

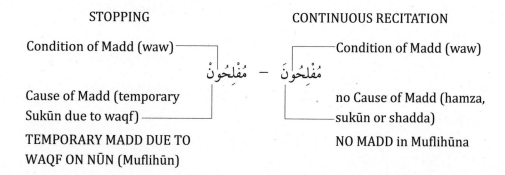

EXAMPLES:

	STOPPING اَلْوَقْفُ		CONTINUOUS اَلْوَصْلُ
Condition of Madd is alif Cause of Madd is bā sākin due to waqf	اَلْكِتَابْ	–	اَلْكِتَابُ
Condition of Madd is waw Cause of Madd is nūn sākin due to waqf	يُنْفِقُونْ	–	يُنْفِقُونَ
Condition of Madd is yā Cause of Madd is mīm sākin due to waqf	اَلرَّجِيمْ	–	اَلرَّجِيمِ

If a temporary sukūn comes after a Līn letter (ـَـ وْ   ـَـ يْ) it is known as Madd 'Āriḍ Līn: اَلْمَدُّ الْعَارِضُ اللِّينُ (Soft Madd):

Madd 'Āriḍ Līn of waw (ـَـ وْ) — نَوْمْ
- Condition of Madd (waw sākin)
- fatha before waw sākin
- Cause of Madd: temporary sukūn due to waqf

Madd 'Āriḍ Līn of yā (ـَـ يْ) — وَالصَّيْفْ
- Condition of Madd (yā sākin)
- fatha before yā sākin
- Cause of Madd: temporary sukūn on fā due to waqf

TABLE 6: SUMMARY OF SECONDARY OR DERIVED MADD مَدٌّ فَرْعِيٌّ

NO.	NAME OF DERIVED MADD	CONDITION OF MADD	CAUSE OF MADD	REMARKS
1	COMPULSORY MADD مَدٌّ وَاجِبٌ (joint Madd مَدٌّ مُتَّصِلٌ)	Sākin letters: Alif, Waw, Yā (ي و ا)	Hamza (ه ا)	Condition of Madd and Cause of Madd must be in the same word.
2	a) PERMISSIBLE MADD مَدٌّ جَائِزٌ (Separated Madd) مَدٌّ مُنْفَصِلٌ	Sākin letters: Alif, Waw, Yā	Hamza	Condition of Madd and Cause of Madd must be in two consecutive words.
	b) PRONUNCIATION RELATED MADD مَدٌّ تَلَفُّظِيٌّ (Elongated Madd مَدٌّ صِلَةٌ)	Sākin yā written as ہِ but pronounced as هِى Sakin waw written as ہُ but pronounced as هُو	Hamza	This is same as permissible Madd but it is given a different name since the condition of Madd is written as ہُ = هُو and ہِ = هِى
3	a) TEMPORARY MADD مَدٌّ عَارِضٌ	Sākin letters: Alif, Waw, Yā	Temporary sukūn due to waqf on a word	If waqf is not made, there will be no Madd
	b) TEMPORARY SOFT MADD (Līn Madd) مَدٌّ عَارِضٌ لِينٌ	Sākin letters: Alif, Waw, Yā	Temporary sukūn due to waqf; the condition of Madd must be preceded by a fatha.	If waqf is not made, there will be no Madd Līn Madd is pronounced softly
4	PERMANENT MADD مَدٌّ لَازِمٌ	Sākin letters: Alif, Waw, Yā	Real sukūn or tashdīd	Tashdīd also has real sukūn since a mushaddad letter is pronounced twice: with sukūn and with haraka
	KALIMĪ MUKHAFFAF كَلِمِيٌّ مُخَفَّفٌ	Sākin letters: Alif, Waw, Yā	Real sukūn	The real sukūn must be in one word
	KALIMĪ MUTHAQQAL كَلِمِيٌّ مُثَقَّلٌ	Sākin letters: Alif, Waw, Yā	Tashdīd	Tashdīd must be in one word
	HARFĪ MUKHAFFAF حَرْفِيٌّ مُخَفَّفٌ	Sākin letters: Alif, Waw, Yā	Real sukūn in pronunciation of an abbreviated letter	The letter sad صٓ is pronounced as صَادْ which contains condition of Madd (alif) and cause of Madd (dal sākin دْ)
	HARFĪ MUTHAQQAL حَرْفِيٌّ مُثَقَّلٌ	Sākin letters: Alif, Waw, Yā	Tashdīd in pronunciation of an abbreviated letter	Tashdīd occurs due to Idgham of one letter into another: الٓمٓ = اَلِفْ لَآمْ مِيم = اَلِفْ لَآمِّيم Condition of Madd (Alif) Cause of Madd (Sukun on mim)

CHAPTER FIVE

THE RULES OF RECITATION

THE RULES OF STOPPING & INITIATION

اَحْكَامُ الْوَقْفِ وَالِابْتِدَاءِ

Waqf (اَلْوَقْفُ) means to stop recitation intentionally to take a new breath or sometimes unintentionally due to sudden coughing, sneezing, or running out of breath during recitation of long verses of the Holy Qur'an. For a proper stop during the recitation, one must know:

- How to stop on a word
- Where to stop in a verse
- How to resume recitation after stopping

HOW TO STOP

During the recitation of the Holy Qur'an, if one needs to stop in the middle or at the end of a verse, the following rules are applied for waqf (stop):

1. SĀKIN LETTER

If the last letter of a word is sākin, then pronounce the sākin letter for waqf:

فَحَدِّثْ

مِنْهُمْ

2. LETTERS OF MADD

If a word ends on any of the letters of Madd (alif, waw, yā), then the letter of the Madd is pronounced:

Pronounced Written

ذِكْرَى – ذِكْرَا

وَاعْبُدُوا – وَعْبُدُو

3. ḤARAKA (VOWEL)

If the last letter of a word has a vowel (fatha, ḍamma, or kasra), then change the vowel by sukūn for waqf:

Pronounced Written

مُنْظَرُونْ – مُنْظَرُونَ

هُو – هُوَ

فِيهْ – فِيهِ

يُمِيتْ – يُمِيتُ

اَطِيعُونْ – اَطِيعُونِ

4. TANWĪN

If the last letter of a word has tanwīn (except double fatha ـً), then the tanwīn is changed into sukūn for waqf:

بِمِقْدَارْ – بِمِقْدَارٍ

شَدِيدْ – شَدِيدٌ

If the last letter of a word has double fatha ـً over any letter (except Tā Mudawwara تَاءٌ مُدَوَّرَةٌ (ة ، ـة) , then double fatha is changed into one fatha (whether there is an extra alif or not) and it is pronounced as Alif Madd:

Pronounced Written

كَبِيرَا – كَبِيرًا

جَمَّا – جَمًّا

نِسَآءَا – نِسَآءً

سُوَى – سُوًى

5. TĀ MUDAWWARA تَاءٌ مُدَوَّرَةٌ (ة ، ـة)

The round tā (ة ، ـة) known as Tā Mudawwara indicates a feminine ending. It may have a ḥaraka or tanwīn on it.

If there is a ḥaraka (fatha, ḍamma, or kasra) on Tā Mudawwara then Tā Mudawwara (ة) is changed into hā sākin (ه) for waqf:

Pronounced Written

بِالرَّحْمَهْ – بِالرَّحْمَةِ

وَالصَّلٰوهْ – وَالصَّلٰوةَ

وَالْاَفْئِدَهْ – وَالْاَفْئِدَةَ

If there is a tanwīn (double fatha, double ḍamma, or double kasra) on Tā Mudawwara, then Tā Mudawwara with tanwīn is changed into hā sākin (هْ) for waqf:

Pronounced Written

ظَالِمَةٌ – ظَالِمَهْ

خَاوِيَةٍ – خَاوِيَهْ

زَكٰوةً – زَكٰوهْ

6. TASHDĪD

A mushaddad letter can have a ḥaraka or a tanwīn on it.

If there is a tashdīd and ḥaraka (fatha, ḍamma, or kasra) on the last letter of a word, then the ḥaraka is changed into sukūn but tashdīd is retained. The pronunciation should be with a force on the sākin letter to indicate a tashdīd on it:

Pronounced Written

فِيهِنَّ – فِيهِنْ ّ/

بِالْحَقِّ – بِالْحَقْ ّ/

اَمَرُّ – اَمَرْ ّ/

If there is a tashdīd and tanwīn (double fatha, double ḍamma, or double kasra) on the last letter of a word, then the tanwīn is changed into sukūn but tashdīd is retained. The pronunciation should be with a force on the sākin letter to indicate the tashdīd:

Pronounced Written

عَرَبِيٌّ – عَرَبِيْ ّ/

خَفِيٌّ – خَفِيْ ّ/

عَدُوٌّ – عَدُوْ ّ/

7. TALAFFUẒĪ WAW AND YĀ

In some words, the letter waw is written as hā with an inverted comma on it:

Pronounced Written

هٗ = هُو

ـهٗ = هُو

The letter yā is also written as hā with a vertical line under it:

Pronounced Written

هِي = هٖ

هِي = ـهٖ

The alternate way of writing waw (هُ) and yā (ـهٖ) is known as Talaffuẓī (Pronunciation related) form of Talaffuẓī waw and Talaffuẓī yā respectively.

If the last letter of a word is either Talaffuẓī waw or Talaffuẓī ya, then it is changed into sākin hā (هْ):

خَلَقَهْ — خَلَقَهُ (Talaffuẓī waw)

لِنَفْسِهْ — لِنَفْسِهٖ (Talaffuẓī yā)

8. NŪN AL-QUTNĪ نُونٌ قُطْنِيٌّ

If there is a sākin letter after the tanwīn, then the nūn of the tanwīn should be given a kasra to connect it with the following sākin letter when it is decided to recite the two words together:

لُمَزَةٍ الَّذِي

- Sākin letter (alif)
- Tanwīn (double kasra)

For waqf on first word:

لُمَزَهْ ○ اَلَّذِي

- Tanwīn is changed into sukūn as per Rule No. 4
- Stop (waqf)
- Haraka (fatha) is given to hamza

For continuous recitation:

lumaza-ti-nil-ladhī = لُمَزَةِ نِ الَّذِي

- Tanwin (double kasra) is changed to Kasra
- The sound of nūn in tanwīn is indicated by nūn with a Kasra

The little nūn with kasra (نِ) is known as Nūn al-Qutnī.

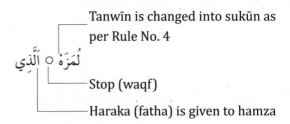

CHART NO. 7 : THE RULES OF STOPPING (WAQF)

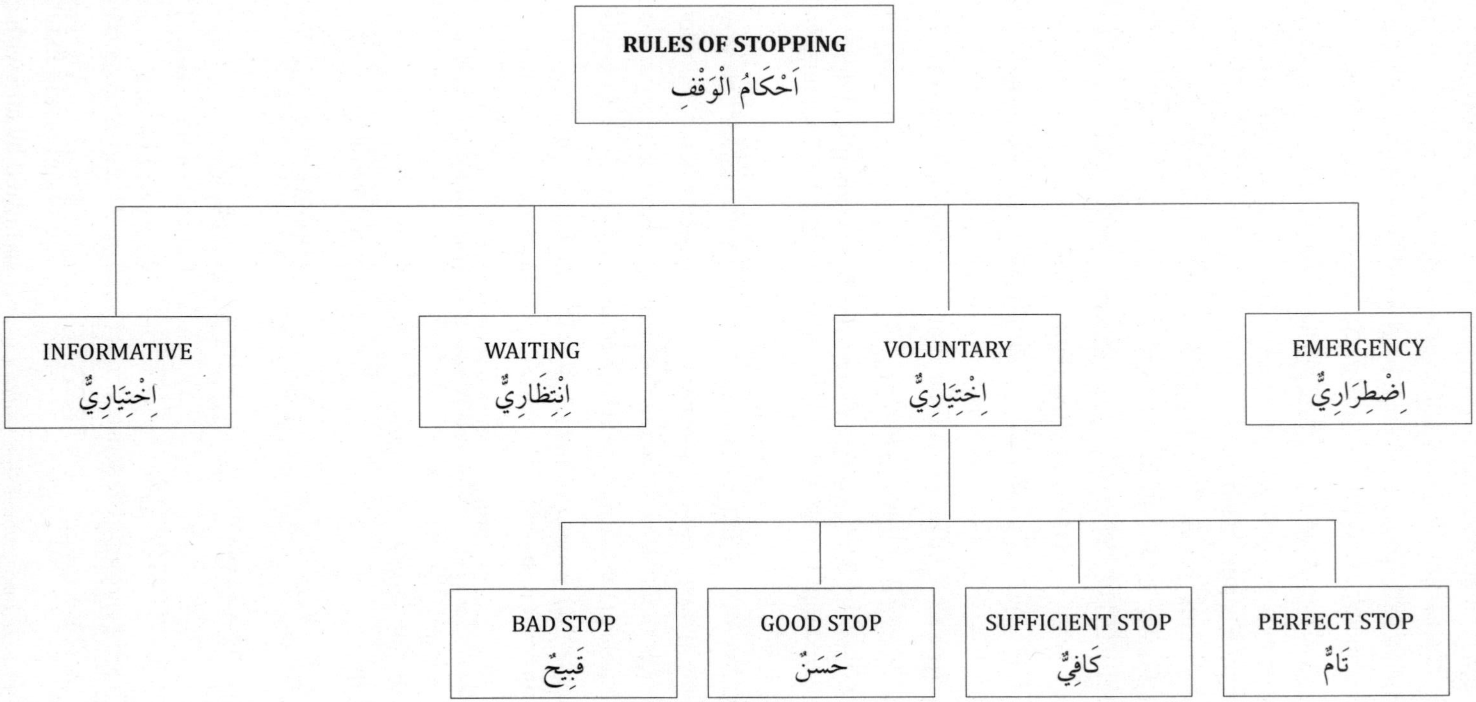

WHERE TO STOP

Normally a stop is made at the end of a verse indicated by a small circle. However, there are other marks within a verse where a waqf is either permitted or there is a warning not to stop at that point. These punctuation marks are explained in detail later in this chapter.

Since most non-Arabic speaking Muslims are not familiar with Arabic grammar, the reciter should try to stop at the end of a verse or at a known punctuation mark where stopping is permitted.

After stopping at a word, the recitation is resumed with a new breath. There are four ways one can make a stop as follows:

1. INFORMATIVE STOP[36] (وَقْفٌ اِخْتِيَارِيٌّ): This is an intentional stop to demonstrate how a waqf is made at any word in a verse.

2. WAITING STOP (وَقْفٌ اِنْتِظَارِيٌّ): Stopping to show the variation in the recitation by seven qirā'a (سَبْعَةُ قِرَاءَة) or ten qirā'a (عَشَرَةُ قِرَاءَة); this occurs when one first recites the qirā'a of shu'ba (شُعْبَة) and then recites it again according to some other qirā'a, say the qirā'a of Ḥafṣ (حَفْص).

3. EMERGENCY STOP (وَقْفٌ اِضْطِرَارِيٌّ): This is an unintentional stopping due to reasons beyond one's control: running out of the breath, coughing, sneezing, sudden interruption, and so on.

4. VOLUNTARY STOP (وَقْفٌ اِخْتِيَارِيٌّ): This is a stop under one's control at the end of a complete sentence, end of a verse, or at any place when it is obvious that a reader will not be able to finish a long verse in one breath. For voluntary stopping, one should select a suitable place taking into account the word as well as its meaning.

There are four ways a voluntary stop can be made:

a) PERFECT STOP (اَلْوَقْفُ التَّامُّ): This is a stop at the end of a verse where the sentence as well as the meaning is complete and there is no connection with the following verse. It is usually at the end of a verse indicated by a small circle (end of verse sign) or at a mandatory stop (وَقْفٌ لَازِمٌ) or at (وَقْفٌ مُطْلَقٌ).

Examples:

بِسْمِ اللهِ الرَّحْمٰنِ الرَّحِيمِ o

اَلْحَمْدُ لِلّٰهِ رَبِّ الْعَالَمِينَ o

b) SUFFICIENT STOP (اَلْوَقْفُ الْكَافِيُّ): This is a stop at a point where the sentence is complete, but the meaning (or sense) is not complete. This generally occurs at the end of a verse. In that case, the initiation (اَلْاِبْتِدَاءُ) is permitted from the next verse.

---

36 Also known as an Instructional Stop where a teacher may stop to show his students how a waqf is made on a particular word or when he is interrupted by his student to ask a question.

Example:

Nay, who is there that can help you, (even as) an army besides (God) Most Merciful?	X	اَمَّنْ هٰذَا الَّذِي هُوَ جُنْدٌ لَّكُمْ يَنْصُرُكُمْ مِنْ دُونِ الرَّحْمٰنِ
In nothing but delusion are the unbelievers. (al-Mulk 67:20)		اِنِ الْكَافِرُونَ اِلَّا فِي غُرُورٍ
SUFFICIENT STOP	:	اَلْوَقْفُ الْكَافِيُّ

c) GOOD STOP (اَلْوَقْفُ الْحَسَنُ): A stop at a point where the sentence or a part of it is complete in meaning but there is something more that follows which has a connection with what is being said.

Example:

لَآ اِلٰهَ اِلَّا هُوَ فَاَنّٰى تُؤْفَكُونَ	X	ذٰلِكُمُ اللهُ رَبُّكُمْ خَالِقُ كُلِّ شَيْءٍ
"There is no god but He: then how ye are deluded away from the Truth!" (al-Ghāfir 40:62)		"Such is God, your Lord, the Creator of all things."
GOOD STOP	:	اَلْوَقْفُ الْحَسَنُ

d) BAD STOP (اَلْوَقْفُ الْقَبِيحُ): This type of stop is not recommended. Here neither the sentence is complete nor the meaning. Sometimes a stop can change the meaning.

Example:

(an-Nisā 4:43) وَاَنْتُمْ سُكَارٰى	X	لَا تَقْرَبُوا الصَّلٰوةَ
"When you are drunk"		"Do not go to the Prayer"
BAD STOP	:	اَلْوَقْفُ الْقَبِيحُ

A stop at the very place marked here will change the meaning, because Prayer is obligatory and stopping at X would distort the intended meaning.

INITIATION AFTER STOP (اَلْاِبْتِدَاءُ)

If one is familiar with the meaning of the verse, then one may resume recitation from an appropriate preceding word which will make a good sense based on the meaning of the word where the waqf was made.

The following general rules are given to initiate recitation after a stop in the middle of a verse.

1. When the recitation is to be resumed from a word beginning with hamzatu'l-waṣl (هَمْزَةُ الْوَصْل), give hamza same ḥaraka (except when it is a fatha) as the one on the third letter of the word:

hamzatu'l-wasl

انْظُرْ – اُنْظُرْ

third letter of the word has a ḍamma ظُ

ḍamma is used to give ḥaraka to hamzatu'l-wasl for initiation

2. If the third letter of the word has a fatha, then hamza is given a kasra:

hamzatu'l-wasl

افْتَحْ – اِفْتَحْ

third letter of the word has a fatha تَ

kasra is used to give ḥaraka to hamzatu'l-wasl for initiation

3. If a word begins with the definite article اَلْ (al-), a fatha is always given to hamza to begin recitation.

hamzatu'l-wasl

الْمَالُ – اَلْمَالُ

word begins with "al-" اَلْ

fatha is given to hamza اَ to pronounce the word

Other Examples:

الَّذِي – اَلَّذِي

الْبَنُونَ – اَلْبَنُونَ

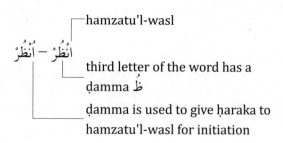

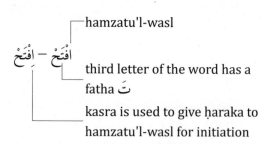

WARNING: The above examples do not give all the rules regarding how to begin reciting from a particular word after waqf. One must know the Arabic language for proper beginning. It is, therefore, always safe to stop at the end of a verse or at a known punctuation mark and resume recitation from a new verse or from a known punctuation mark where waqf is allowed.

4. The recitation of the Holy Qur'an must begin with Ta'awwudh (تَعَوُّذ) as commanded by Allah:

﴿فَاِذَا قَرَأْتَ الْقُرْآنَ فَاسْتَعِذْ بِاللهِ مِنَ الشَّيْطَانِ الرَّجِيمِ﴾

"When you read the Qur'an, seek Allah's protection from Satan the rejected one." (an-Nahl 16 : 98)

Ta'awwudh is to say: اَعُوذُ بِاللهِ مِنَ الشَّيْطَانِ الرَّجِيمِ

(which means, "I seek Allah's protection from Satan the rejected one.")

With the exception of Sūra at-Tawba, every sūra is prefixed with Basmalah (اَلْبَسْمَلَة):

بِسْمِ اللهِ الرَّحْمٰنِ الرَّحِيمِ

(which means, "In the Name of Allah, the All-Merciful, the All-Compassionate.")

Therefore, a reciter must begin a sūra, first reciting Ta'awwudh and then Basmalah. The following chart shows four permitted ways to begin with Ta'awwudh, Basmalah, and the Sūra to be recited.

TABLE 7 : THE RECITATION OF TA'AWWUDH AND BASMALAH

No.	Ta'awwudh	O = Stop → = No Stop	Basmalah	O = Stop → = No Stop	Sûra
	تَعَوُّذ	اَلْوَقْف→اَلْوَصْل	بَسْمَلَة	اَلْوَقْف→اَلْوَصْل	سُورَة
1	اَعُوذُ بِاللهِ مِنَ الشَّيْطَانِ الرَّجِيمْ	O	بِسْمِ اللهِ الرَّحْمٰنِ الرَّحِيمْ	O	قُلْ هُوَ اللهُ اَحَدٌ
2	اَعُوذُ بِاللهِ مِنَ الشَّيْطَانِ الرَّجِيمِ	→	بِسْمِ اللهِ الرَّحْمٰنِ الرَّحِيمِ	→	قُلْ هُوَ اللهُ اَحَدٌ
3	اَعُوذُ بِاللهِ مِنَ الشَّيْطَانِ الرَّجِيمِ	→	بِسْمِ اللهِ الرَّحْمٰنِ الرَّحِيمْ	O	قُلْ هُوَ اللهُ اَحَدٌ
4	اَعُوذُ بِاللهِ مِنَ الشَّيْطَانِ الرَّجِيمْ	O	بِسْمِ اللهِ الرَّحْمٰنِ الرَّحِيمِ	→	قُلْ هُوَ اللهُ اَحَدٌ

EXPLANATION OF TABLE 7

1. Recite Ta'awwudh, Basmalah, and Sūra all separately making stop (waqf) in between.
2. Recite Ta'awwudh, Basmalah, and Sūra together without stop (waqf) in between.
3. Recite Ta'awwudh and Basmalah together then stop (waqf); recite Sūra after stop.
4. Recite Ta'awwudh then stop (waqf); recite Basmalah and sūra together without any stop after Basmalah.

5. Recitation of Basmalah Between Two Sūras: With the exception of Sūra at-Tawba, one can recite Basmalah, between two sūras of the Holy Qur'an in one of the three ways as shown in the following chart.

TABLE 8 : THE RECITATION OF BASMALAH BETWEEN TWO SŪRAS

No.	End of a Sūra	O = Stop → = No Stop	Basmalah	O = Stop → = No Stop	Start of a New Sūra
1	وَلَمْ يَكُنْ لَهُ كُفُوًا اَحَدٌ	O	بِسْمِ اللهِ الرَّحْمٰنِ الرَّحِيمِ	O	قُلْ اَعُوذُ بِرَبِّ الْفَلَقِ
2	وَلَمْ يَكُنْ لَهُ كُفُوًا اَحَدٌ	→	بِسْمِ اللهِ الرَّحْمٰنِ الرَّحِيمِ	→	قُلْ اَعُوذُ بِرَبِّ الْفَلَقِ
3	وَلَمْ يَكُنْ لَهُ كُفُوًا اَحَدٌ	O	بِسْمِ اللهِ الرَّحْمٰنِ الرَّحِيمِ	→	قُلْ اَعُوذُ بِرَبِّ الْفَلَقِ

EXPLANATION OF TABLE 8

1. Stop (waqf) before and after Basmalah
2. Do not stop (waqf) before and after Basmalah
3. Stop (waqf) before Basmalah and not after it.

Note: It is not permitted to recite the last verse of the sūra together with Basmalah and then stop. This will give the impression that Basmalah is a part of the sūra. In fact, it is always written at the top of each sūra, except Sūra at-Tawba.

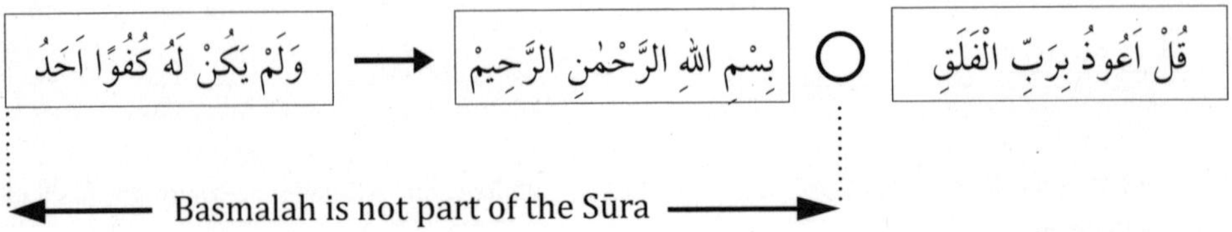

THE PAUSE OR SAKTA

اَلسَّكْتَةُ

A pause while not breaking the breath in the recitation of the Holy Qur'an is called Sakta (اَلسَّكْتَةُ). It is equivalent to English comma. The following are the places in the Holy Qur'an where Sakta occurs.

Al-Kahf 18:1–2

﴿وَلَمْ يَجْعَل لَّهُ عِوَجَا ۜ قَيِّمًا لِّيُنذِرَ﴾

Yā-Sīn 36:52

﴿قَالُوا يَا وَيْلَنَا مَن بَعَثَنَا مِن مَّرْقَدِنَا ۜ هَٰذَا مَا
وَعَدَ الرَّحْمَٰنُ وَصَدَقَ الْمُرْسَلُونَ﴾

Al-Qiyāmah 75:27[37]

﴿وَقِيلَ مَنْ ۜ رَاقٍ﴾

Al-Muṭaffifīn 83:14[38]

﴿كَلَّا بَلْ ۜ رَانَ﴾

[37] Due to Sakta between مَنْ and رَاقٍ, there is no Idghām of nūn sakīn, although the conditions of Idghām without nasalization are met.

[38] Due to Sakta between بَلْ and رَانَ, there is no Idghām of the letter lām into rā, although the conditions of Idghām of two close makhraj letters have been met.

THE PUNCTUATION MARKS

عَلَامَاتُ الضَّبْطِ

When we speak, our gestures and tone of voice or intonation[39] help us put our meaning across. When we write, the punctuation we use is a guide to our meaning. The Qur'anic punctuation is an elaborate system in which three kinds of marks are used.

1. VARIATION IN RECITATION

The most common mark to show the variation in the system of Qirā'a is known as Mu'ānaqa (اَلْمُعَانَقَة).[40] A certain word or expression enclosed within three dots (∴) can be understood as going either with the words or expressions preceding it or with those following it. In the margin is printed مع where it was worked out by the earliest commentators known as اَلْمُتَقَدِّمِين or the word مُعَانَقَة where it was worked out by the later commentators known as اَلْمُتَأَخِّرِين. The idea of using the three dots is taken from the word مُعَانَقَة itself which contains three dots; one is nūn ن and two in qāf ق.

An example of Mu'ānaqa can be found in Sūra al-Baqara 2:2, where the word fīhi فِيهِ is enclosed within three dots (∴ فِيهِ ∴). The reciter can make a stop (waqf) either at the first occurrence of three dots or at the second occurrence of three dots. In either case the meaning will be perfectly clear.

STOP AT THE FIRST OCCURRENCE OF THREE DOTS

﴿ذَٰلِكَ الْكِتَابُ لَا رَيْبَ * فِيهِ هُدًى لِّلْمُتَّقِينَ﴾

This is the Book without a doubt | STOP | In it is guidance to those who fear God

---

[39] "Intonation" is the rise and fall in the pitch of the voice in speech which contributes to the total meaning of an utterance.

[40] Also known as Murāqabah اَلْمُرَاقَبَة.

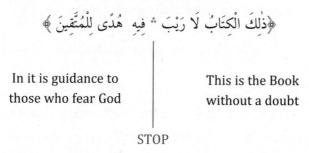

STOP AT THE SECOND OCCURRENCE OF THREE DOTS

﴿ ذٰلِكَ الْكِتَابُ لَا ۛ رَيْبَ ۛ فِيهِ هُدًى لِلْمُتَّقِينَ ﴾

Guidance to those who fear God		This is the Book without a doubt in it
	STOP	

The reciter should not stop at both places, i.e. before and after فِيهِ , since it will not make any sense in meaning.

2. MARGINAL MARKS

The marks used in the margins of the copies of the Qur'an are as follows:

AR-RUBA' (OR HIZB)	اَلرُّبُعُ	:	One fourth of the juz
AN-NISF	اَلنِّصْفُ	:	One half of the juz
ATH-THALĀTHA	اَلثَّلٰثَةُ	:	Three fourth of the juz
AS-SAJDA	اَلسَّجْدَةُ	:	Indication that the verse requires a recitational prostration.

3. PUNCTUATION MARKS

There are ordinary punctuation marks in the text of the Holy Qur'an are as follows:

WAQF TĀMM وَقْفٌ تَامٌّ: It is the most important of all and indicates the end of one verse and the beginning of the next one. The ending of a Kūfī verse is indicated by "O" while a non-Kūfī verse ending is expressed by the symbol of "ه". An example of non-Kūfī verse can be found in (non 'Uthmanic text of) the Qur'an (1:6):

صِرَاطَ الَّذِينَ اَنْعَمْتَ عَلَيْهِمْ ه غَيْرِ الْمَغْضُوبِ عَلَيْهِمْ وَلَا الضَّالِّينَ

لا (LĀ): A warning not to stop.

م (WAQF LĀZIM) وَقْفٌ لَازِمٌ : (A stop is absolutely necessary otherwise the sense is spoilt. This is so important that it is also shown prominently in the margin as mandatory stop.

ط (MUṬLAQ) مُطْلَقٌ : (Denotes a full stop, i.e. the end of the sentence, but not the end of an argument.

ج (JĀ'IZ) جَائِزٌ : A stop is optional, but if you do not stop, the sense is not spoilt.

ز (TAJĀWAZ) تَجَاوَزٌ : It is better to pass here than to stop.

ص (MURAKH-KHAṢ) مُرَخَّصٌ : May stop here or continue by connecting to the next word.

صلى (AL-WAṢL 'AWLA) اَلْوَصْلُ اَوْلَى : Should join with what follows.

ق (QĪLA 'ALAIHI'L-WAQF) قِيلَ عَلَيْهِ الْوَقْفِ : May stop but preferred to join with the following word.

صل (QAD YŪṢAL) قَدْ يُوصَلُ : A stop is optional.

قِفْ (QIF) To stop here but if continued, sense is not spoilt.

ك (KADHĀLIK) كَذٰلِكَ : Follow the punctuation mark which preceded it.

س / سكته (SAKTA) سَكْتَةٌ : A stop of the voice (or sound) for a few seconds be made without renewing the breath when continuing. It is necessary to continue and undesirable to stop here.

لا O When one mark is put on the top of the other, then either one could be followed. However, preference is given to the symbol that appears on the top.

THE METHODS OF RECITATION

اَلْمَرَاتِبُ التِّلاَوَة

The Holy Qur'an may be recited acceptably in any one of the following three ways.

1. TARTĪL[41] اَلتَّرتِيل

This method of recitation is to give every letter its correct articulation, observing all qualities of letters and following all rules of Tajwīd, including:

- being careful to give long vowels their full length
- clearly pronouncing a letter from its proper place of articulation
- giving the short vowels full utterance
- keeping the single letters single, double letters double (tashdīd)
- allowing nasalized letters their proper nasalization (ghunna)
- avoiding any shortening (qaṣr)
- observing the rules of nūn sakīn and tanwīn: Iẓhār, idghām, Ikhfā', and Iqlāb
- giving each letter its proper quality

This is the method mentioned in Qur'an:

﴿وَرَتِّلِ الْقُرْآنَ تَرْتِيلاً﴾

And recite the Qur'an with tartīl: in slow, measured rhythmic tone. (Al-Muzzammil 73:4)

2. ḤADR اَلْحَدْرُ

In this method, the verses are recited hastily, though not solvently. It takes advantage of all opportunities for shortening قَصْرٌ , lightening تَفْخِيمٌ , omitting vowels اِسْكَانٌ, slighting اِخْتِلَاصٌ , substitution بَدَلٌ , merger اِدْغَامٌ , lightening the glottal stop هَمْزَةٌ , and so on.

This method is said to add much beauty to the recitation as well as making it easier than Tartīl. According to a report, the Prophet said:

41 Also known as Tahqīq.

Whosoever recites a single letter of the Book of Allah will have a good deed credited to him, and the reward of any good deed will be multiplied by ten. (At-Tirmidhi, Sunan)

It was in this connection that this method was developed, so more quickly one reads the more one could read and thereby have more (rewards for their) good deeds.

3. TADWĪR التَّدْوِيرُ

This method of recitation is midway between labored articulation of Tartīl and hurried articulation of Ḥadr. Tadwīr means "to set in stately measure and adorn with the melodies لُحُونٌ and chants اَصْوَاتٌ of the Arabic language," thus beautifying the sound and tones as far as it is feasible.

The use of the following in the recitation of the Holy Qur'an is strongly discouraged:

1.	k	ك	pronounced like	g	(as in good)
2.	j	ج	pronounced like	k	ك
3.	j	ج	pronounced like	sh	ش
4.	ḍ	ض	pronounced like	d	د
5.	ṣ	ص	pronounced like	s	س
6.	ṭ	ط	pronounced like	t	ت
7.	ẓ	ظ	pronounced like	th	ث or like z ز
8.	b	ب	pronounced like	f	ف

The use of the following is tolerated in the recitation of the Holy Qur'an:

1. The slightly nasalized nūn
2. The hamza ء halfway articulated
3. The long vowel, ā, articulated sharply
4. The letter ḍād ض which sounds like zay ز

THE RECOGNIZED VERSIONS OF THE RECITATION

The Holy Qur'an is generally recited according to any one of the recognized versions of recitation left behind by the well known reciters of the Qur'an. The first seven names listed in Table 9 are the reciters whose recitation came to be known as سَبْعَةُ قِرَاءَاتٍ , when all ten different versions are taken together it is known as عَشَرَةُ قِرَاءَاتٍ.

It is reported that 'Āṣim ibn Abī'n-Najud at-Tabi'i al-Kūfī (عَاصِم بِن اَبِي النَّجُود التَّابِعِي الْكُوفِي) learned the recitation of the Qur'an from Abī 'Abdullah bin Habīb as-Sulamī, who learned it from 'Uthman bin 'Affan (the third Caliph), 'Ali ibn Abī Tālib (the fourth Caliph), Zaid bin Thābit and Ubayy bin Ka'ab (two well known scribes of the Prophet), who learned it directly from the Prophet.[42]

42 رواه حفص بن سليمان بن المغيرة الاسدى الكوفي لقراءة عاصم بن ابي النجود الكوفي التابعي عن ابي عبد الرحمن عبد الله بن حبيب السلمي عن عثمان بن عفان رضي الله عنه وعلي بن ابي طالب وزيد بن ثابت وابي بن كعب رضوان الله عليهم عن النبي صلى الله عليه وسلم.

TABLE 9: TEN RECOGNIZED RECITERS OF THE QUR'AN

NO	NAME OF THE QĀRI	PLACE & DATE OF DEATH
1.	NĀFI 'AL-MADANĪ نَافعُ الْمَدَنِي	MADĪNA, 169 AH / 785 CE
2.	IBN KATHĪR AL-MAKKĪ AT-TABI'Ī اِبْنُ كَثِير الْمَكِّي التَّابعِي	MAKKA, 120 AH / 738 CE
3.	ABŪ 'AMR BIN 'AMMĀR AL-BASRĪ اَبُو عُمَر بِن عَمَّار البَصرِي	KŪFA, 153 AH / 770 CE
4.	'ABDULLAH BIN 'AMIR ASH-SHĀMĪ عَبْدُ اللهِ ابنِ عامِرِ الشَّامِي	DAMASCUS, 188 AH / 736 CE
5.	'ASIM BIN HABĪB AT-TABI'Ī AL-KŪFĪ عَاصِم بنِ حَبِيب اَبِي النَّجُودِ التَّابِعِي الكُوفِي	KŪFA, 127 AH / 744 CE
6.	HAMZA BIN HABĪB AZ-ZAYYĀT AL-KŪFĪ حَمْزَة بنِ حَبِيب الزَّيَّاتِ الكُوفِي	HALWĀN, 156 AH / 773 CE
7.	'ALI BIN HAMZA AL-KASA'Ī AL-KŪFĪ عَلِي بنِ حَمْزَةَ الكَسَائِي الكُوفِي	NEAR AR-RI, 189 AH / 805 CE
8.	ABŪ JA'FAR AL-MADANĪ (YAZID BIN AL-QA'QA') اَبُو جَعْفَر المَدَني (يَزِيد بن القَعقَاع)	MADĪNA, 132 AH / 750 CE
9.	YA'QŪB AL-BASRĪ يَعقُوبِ البَصْرِي	BASRA, 205 AH / 820 CE
10.	KHALAF BIN HISHĀM AL-BAZZĀR AL-BAGHDADĪ خَلَف بن هِشَام الْبَزَار الْبَغْدَادِي	BAGHDĀD, 229 AH / 843 CE

THE ABBREVIATED LETTERS

اَلْحُرُوفُ الْمُقَطَّعَاتُ

Certain sūras have certain letters of the alphabet prefixed to them which are called اَلْحُرُوفُ الْمُقَطَّعَاتُ (Abbreviated Letters). They are always included in the text of the Holy Qur'an and recited as a part of it. These letters are pronounced separately although they are written as words. In the Holy Qur'an published in Arab countries, the Abbreviated Letters ḥā ح , rā ر , ṭā ط , hā هـ , and yā ي have no vertical lines over them as a replacement for Alif.

In fact, there is no need for such an Alif to be placed over these letters since the Arabic names for these letters are حَا ، رَا ، طَا ، هَا and يَا respectively. The Abbreviated Letters Ṭā- Hā طه (prefixed to sūra 20) should not be taken as a word or to be written as طٰهٰ. The letter mīm م when preceded by lām ل or sīn س, should not have tashdīd on it, as in the following Abbreviated Letters:

الٓمّٓ	should be written as	الٓمٓ
الٓمّٓرٰ	should be written as	الٓمٓرٰ
الٓمّٓصٓ	should be written as	الٓمٓصٓ
طٰسٓمّٓ	should be written as	طٰسٓمٓ

A complete list of Abbreviated Letters together with their correct written form and pronunciation is given in Table 10.

MEANINGS OF THE ABBREVIATED LETTERS

At present we do not know as to their exact meanings. Opinions differ as to their significance although a number of commentators have offered opinions to explain their meaning and significance.

A few of these opinions by the commentators are given for the reader to understand what they have to say.

Syed Abul A'la Maududi[43] presents the following explanation regarding the meaning of the Abbreviated Letters:

---

[43] Maududi, *Tafhim-ul-Qur'an*, Vol. 1, Islamic Publications Ltd., Lahore, Pakistan. First Edition 1967.

> Letters of the Arabic alphabet like Alif Lām Mīm الٓمٓ which are prefixed to a number of sūras of the Qur'an, were in common use in the Arabic literature of the period when the Qur'an was revealed. The poets and rhetoricians made use of this style, and instances of this use can be found in the pre-Islamic prose and poetry which has survived. As their significance was appreciated by all concerned, none objected to or questioned about their use, because it was no enigma[44] to them. Even the bitterest opponents of the Qur'an, who never missed an opportunity, did not raise any objection against their use. But as their use was abandoned with the passage of time, it became difficult for the commentators to determine their exact meaning and significance.

'Abdullah Yusuf 'Ali[45] on his discussion of the Abbreviated Letters explained his view as follows:

> Mystic meaning, not intelligible at first sight, is not inconsistent with the character of the Qur'an as a 'Plain Book'. The book of nature is also a plain book, but how few can fully understand it? Everyone can get out of the Qur'an's plain guidance for his life according to his capacity for spiritual understanding. This is not a mystery of the same class as 'mysteries' by which we are asked to believe against the dictates of reason. If we are asked to believe one is three and three is one, we can give no intelligible meanings to the words. If we are asked to believe that certain initials have a meaning which will be understood in the fullness of time or of spiritual development, we are asked to draw upon Faith, but we are not asked to do any violence to our reason.

He further presents a detailed explanation of the Abbreviated Letters Alif Lām Mīm of Sūra al-Baqara as follows:

> Much has been written about the meaning of these letters, but most of it is pure conjecture...Among the conjectures there are two plausible theories. One is that each initial represents an attribute of God. Among the attribute it is not difficult to select three which will fit in with these three letters (Alif Lām Mīm). Another theory, favored by Baidhawi, is that these three letters are the initial, final and middle (or again the initial) letters of three names: Allah, Jibril, and Muhammad, the source of revelation, the heavenly messenger who brought it, and the human Messenger through whom it was promulgated in human speech. This might be appropriate to the first sūra (which al-Baqara really is, if we treat al-Fatiha as a preface) but it was prefixed to others, why to these six only?[46]
>
> If we look to the nature of the sounds which the letters represent, Alif is a breathing and comes from the throat, Lām is a lingual-palatal-dental sound from the middle of the mouth, and Mīm is a labial or lip sound. Can we not take them as symbolical of the beginning, middle, and the end? If so, are they not appropriate to the sūras which treat specifically of Life, Growth, and Death; the beginning and the end? In the New Testaments of Greek scripture, the first and the last letters of the Greek alphabet, Alpha and Omega, are symbolic of the beginning and the end, and give one of the title of God: 'I am Alpha and Omega, the Beginning and the Ending, said the Lord, which is, and which was, and which is to come, the Almighty.' (Rev. 1:8). This symbolism of three things is better with three letters.

---

44 An obscure speech or writing; something hard to understand or explain.

45 Yusuf Ali, *The Holy Qur'an, Text, Translation, and Commentary.*

46 Reference is to letters Alif Lām Mīm that are found prefixed to six sūras in all: 2, 3, 29, 30, 31, 32.

Yet another explanation given by 'Abdullah Yusuf 'Ali is as follows:

> There are 29 letters in the Arabic alphabet, (counting Hamza and Alif as two letters), and there are twenty nine sūras which have abbreviated letters prefixed to them. If we take the half of the alphabet, omitting the fraction, we get 14, and this is the number of letters which actually occur in the Muqatta'at. . . The science of phonetics tells us that our vocal sound arise from the expulsion of air from the lungs, and the sounds are determined by the way in which breath passes through the various organs of speech, e.g., the throat (guttural), or the various positions of the tongue to the middle or to the front of the palate or to the teeth, or the plays of lips. Everyone of these kinds of sounds is presented in these letters.

The same commentator[47] gives the following mystic interpretation of sūras 7 (al-A'rāf), 19 (Maryam), 38 (Sād), beginning with كٓهيٰعٓصٓ ، الٓمٓصٓ and صٓ respectively.

> The factor common to sūra VII [7], sūra XIX [19], and sūra XXXVIII [38], is that in each case the core of the sūra consists of the stories (Qiṣāṣ) of the prophets. In this sūra VII we have the stories of Noah, Hud, Sālih, Lot, Shu'aib, and Moses, leading upto Muhammad, and in Sūra XXXVIII the stories of David, Solomon, and Job similarly lead upto Muhammad, occupying three out of the five sections. Sūra XIX consists almost entirely of such stories. Can we understand Ṣād to stand for qiṣaṣ, of which it is the most characteristic letter?

The commentator, Abdullah Yusuf Ali, finally concludes:

> But no one can be dogmatic about these symbols. We must accept them as symbols with mystic meaning.

Amīn Aḥsan Islahī[48] quoted his ustad (teacher), Farahī, who suggested another but different explanation as to the meaning and significance of the Abbreviated Letters. His interested reasoning is based on historical fact that the pictures were first developed to express the meaning. The Egyptian art of hieroglyphics is an example to this effect. He gives an example of sūra Ṭā-Hā طٰهٰ , which according to him appears to be a symbol for snake and this sūra describes the magicians' snakes which were swallowed by Moses' staff.

In conclusion, the above views strengthen the reasoning of Maududī that these Abbreviated Letters were never a new thing to the polytheist Arabs; they were familiar with them and thus none ever raised an eyebrow or frowned as to their meanings.

Finally, Maududī asked a simple question that is of great value to an ordinary reader:

> Should an ordinary reader be concerned with the significance and meanings of the Abbreviated Letters to obtain guidance and understanding from the Qur'an?

---

[47] Ibid, p. 341, note 989 (Sūra Ṣād).

[48] Islahi, Amin Ahsan. *Tadabbur al-Qur'an.*

TABLE 10: THE ABBREVIATED LETTERS WITH PRONUNCIATION

اَلْحُرُوفُ الْمُقَطَّعَاتُ

NO.	NAME OF THE SŪRA		SŪRA NUMBER	NUMBER OF ABBREVIATED LETTERS	ABBREVIATED LETTERS		PRONUNCIATION
1.	ṢĀD	صٓ	38	ONE	صٓ	(صَادْ)	ṢĀD
	QĀF	قٓ	50		قٓ	(قَافْ)	QĀF
	QALAM	اَلْقَلَمُ	68		نٓ	(نُونْ)	NŪN
2.	ṬĀ HĀ	طٰهٰ	20	TWO	طٰهٰ	(طَاهَا)	ṬĀ HĀ
	NAML	اَلنَّمْلُ	27		طٰسٓ	(طَاسِينْ)	ṬĀ SĪN
	YĀ SĪN	يٰسٓ	36		يٰسٓ	(يَاسِينْ)	YĀ SĪN
	MU'MIN	اَلْمُؤْمِنُ	40				
	HĀ MĪM	حٰمٓ	41*		حٰمٓ	(حَامِيمْ)	HĀ MĪM
	SHŪRĀ	اَلشُّورٰى	42				
	ZUKHRUF	اَلزُّخْرُفُ	43				
	DUKHĀN	اَلدُّخَانُ	44				
	JĀTHIA	اَلجَاثِيَةُ	45				
	AHQĀF	اَلْاَحْقَافُ	46				
3.	BAQARA	اَلْبَقَرَةُ	2	THREE			
	ĀL ʻIMRĀN	اٰل عِمْرَان	3				
	ʻANKABŪT	اَلْعَنْكَبُوتُ	29		الٓمٓ	(اَلِفْ لَامْ مِيمْ)	ALIF-LĀM-MĪM
	RŪM	اَلرُّومُ	30				
	LUQMĀN	لُقْمَانُ	31				
	SAJDA	اَلسَّجْدَةُ	32				
	YŪNUS	يُونُسُ	10				
	HŪD	هُودُ	11				
	YŪSUF	يُوسُفُ	12		الٓرٰ	(اَلِفْ لَامْ رَا)	ALIF LĀM RĀ
	IBRAHĪM	اِبْرٰهِيمُ	14				
	HIJR	اَلْحِجْرُ	15				
	SHUʻARĀ	اَلشُّعَرَاءُ	26		طٰسٓمٓ	(طَاسِيمِّيمْ)	ṬĀ SĪM-MĪM
4.	QAṢAṢ	اَلْقَصَصُ	28	FOUR			
	ʻARĀF	اَلْاَعْرَافُ	7		الٓمٓصٓ	(اَلِفْ لَامِّيمْ صَادْ)	ALIF LĀM MĪM SĀD
	RAʻD	اَلرَّعْدُ	13		الٓمٓرٰ	(اَلِفْ لَامِّيمْ رَا)	ALIF LĀM MĪM RĀ
5.	MARYAM	مَرْيَمُ	19	FIVE	كٓهٰيٰعٓصٓ	(كَافْ هَايَاعَينْ صَادْ)	KĀF HĀ YĀ ʻAIN SĀD
	SHŪRĀ	اَلشُّورٰى	42*		حٰمٓ عٓسٓقٓ	(حَامِيمْ، عَينْ سِينْ قَافْ)	HĀ MĪM ʻAIN SĪN QĀF

* Sūra No. 42 is included in Two Abbreviated letters series as well as in Five Abbreviated letters series.

Chapter Six

MOST COMMON ERRORS

COMMONLY MISPRONOUNCED WORDS

Certain words are used very frequently in the Holy Qur'an. A non-Arabic speaking reader quickly becomes familiar due to their repeated occurrences. However, when the same words are occasionally used with a slight change of fatha, ḍamma, or kasra, the tendency is to pronounce them also like the ones occurring frequently, thereby changing the meanings.

An attempt is made here to present a list of such commonly mispronounced words and phrases. To derive the optimum benefit, it is recommended that the reader should mark all such places in the margin of his personal copy of the Qur'an. This will caution the reader to take special care in the pronunciation and observance of the noticeable difference from that of the familiar usage.

1. THUMMA ثُمَّ AND ثَمَّ THAMMA

The word *thumma* ثُمَّ (with a ḍamma on thā ث) occurs frequently in the Holy Qur'an. But the word *thamma* ثَمَّ (with a fatha on thā ثَ) occurs only at four places. Here the tendency is to read the word *thamma* (with fatha) ثَمَّ as *thumma* (with ḍamma) ثُمَّ. Care should be taken to retain fatha on thā ثَ at the following four places in Qur'an:

QUR'AN 2:115	فَثَمَّ وَجْهُ اللهِ
QUR'AN 26:64	ثَمَّ الْاٰخَرِينَ
QUR'AN 76:20	ثَمَّ رَأَيْتَ نَعِيمًا
QUR'AN 81:21	ثَمَّ أَمِينٍ

2. AYYUHĀ أَيُّهَا AND AYYUHA أَيُّهَ

The word AYYUHĀ (ending with hā alif هَا) أَيُّهَا is found at many places in the Qur'an, but the word AYYUHA (ending with ha with fatha ـهَ) أَيُّهَ occurs at the following three places:

QUR'AN 24:31	أَيُّهَ الْمُؤْمِنُونَ
QUR'AN 43:49	يَا أَيُّهَ السَّاحِرُ
QUR'AN 55:31	أَيُّهَ الثَّقَلَانِ

The reader should take special care in pronouncing Ayyuha أَيُّهَ so as not to lengthen fatha on ha to the extent of alif as in أَيُّهَا .

3. YASHĀ ALLAH يَشَآءَ اللهُ AND YASHA ILLAH يَشَاءِ اللهُ

Usually there is a fatha on hamza ءَ in Yashā' يَشَآءَ except at the following places where it has kasra on hamza in Yashā' يَشَاءِ.

QUR'AN 6:39	مَنْ يَشَاءِ اللهُ
QUR'AN 42:24	فَإِنْ يَشَاءِ اللهُ

4. YAW-MA'ZIN يَوْمَئِذٍ AND YAW-MI'ZIN يَوْمِئِذٍ

The word Yaw-ma'zin يَوْمَئِذٍ occurs frequently in the Qur'an, whereas the word Yaw-mi'zin يَوْمِئِذٍ is found at the following two places:

QUR'AN 11:66	وَمِنْ خِزْيِ يَوْمِئِذٍ
QUR'AN 70:11	مِنْ عَذَابِ يَوْمِئِذٍ

5. The following table lists single occurrences of words:

These words are written with a slight change of vowel (fatha, ḍamma, or kasra).

COMMON OCCURRENCE	EXCEPTION TO COMMON OCCURRENCE	REMARKS
تَحْتِهَا الْأَنْهَارُ Tahti hal Anhāru	تَحْتَهَا الْأَنْهَارُ Tahta hal Anhāru (Qur'an 9:100)	Usually the second ت has kasra; exception is the Tā ت with fatha.
وَنِعْمَةٍ wa ni'matin	وَنَعْمَةٍ wa na'matin (Qur'an 44:27)	Usually the nūn ن has kasra; exception is the Nūn ن with fatha.
الْمُخْلِصِينَ Al-Mukhli-sīna	الْمُخْلَصِينَ Al-Mukhla-sīna (Qur'an 44:27)	Usually the lām ل has kasra; exception is the Lām ل with fatha.

اَلَّذِى Al-Ladhī	قَسَمٌ لِذِى Al-Lidhī (Qur'an 89:5)	Lām ل with fatha everywhere; exception is Lām ل with kasra
اَلَّذِينَ Al-Ladhīni	اَرِنَا الَّذَيْنِ Al-Ladhaini (Qur'an 41:29)	Usually dhāl ذ has kasra with the exception of having fatha here.
مُسْلِمِينَ Muslimīna	وَاجْعَلْنَا مُسْلِمَيْنِ Muslimaini (Qur'an 2:128)	Nūn ن in this word has fatha everywhere with the exception of having kasra here.
مُؤْمِنِينَ Mu'minīna	اَبَوٰهُ مُؤْمِنَيْنِ Mu'minaini (Qur'an 18:80)	Nūn ن in this word has fatha everywhere with the exception of having kasra here.
خَالِدِينَ Khalidīna	اَنَّهُمَا فِي النَّارِ خَالِدَيْنِ Khalidaini (Qur'an 59:17)	Nūn ن in this word has fatha everywhere with the exception of having kasra here.

6. The following table gives those words that are mispronounced due to failure to carefully observe ḥaraka, sukūn or tashdīd:

WORDS / PHRASES	TYPE OF ERRORS
يَوْمِ الْجُمُعَةِ (Qur'an 62:9)	Refrain from pronouncing Jumu'a جُمُعَة as Juma'a جُمَعَة (mīm with fatha instead of ḍamma) or as Jama'a جَمَعَة (jīm ج and mīm م with fatha instead of ḍamma)
اِلًّا وَلَا ذِمَّةً (Qur'an 9:8)	Note tanwīn (double fatha) on اِلًّا here, and do not pronounce it as Illā اِلَّا which occurs frequently.
وَهُوَ كَلٌّ عَلٰى مَوْلٰهُ (Qur'an 16:76)	Observe fatha on كَلٌّ (kallun) as opposed to frequently occuring with ḍamma: كُلٌّ (kullun).
اِحْدَى الْحُسْنَيَيْنِ (Qur'an 9:52)	Note that there are two ya's occuring one after the other; first one is with fatha and the second with sukūn.
وُكِّلَ بِكُمْ (Qur'an 32:11)	There is a tashdīd on وُكِّلَ ; it is to be pronounced as wukkila instead of hurriedly pronounced as wu-kila وُكِلَ (kāf without tashdīd)

وَقَالَتِ الْيَهُودُ عُزَيْرٌ ابْنُ اللهِ (Qur'an 9:30)	The word عُزَيْرٌ has ḍamma on the letter of rā; it is to be pronounced as 'Uzairu-nib-nullah (rā with ḍamma) instead of 'Uzair-nib-nullah (rā with sukūn)
وَجِاۤىءَ (Qur'an 89:23)	Alif is unsounded (سَاقِطٌ) and it is pronounced as wa-jīa'.

7. Frequent errors are also made due to incorrect pronunciation of words containing mushaddad letters.

A mushaddad letter is always pronounced twice; first with sukūn with the preceding letter and then with ḥaraka (fatha, ḍamma, kasra) or tanwīn with the following letter. In case of mushaddad emphatic letters (ظ ، ط ، ض ، ص) pronunciation becomes more difficult and requires practice to master it.

In the following words, observe tashdīd and pronounce them carefully:

QUR'AN 37:62	شَجَرَةَ الزَّقُّومِ
QUR'AN 30:43	يَصَّدَّعُونَ
QUR'AN 36:49	يَخِصِّمُونَ
QUR'AN 37:8	يَسَّمَّعُونَ
QUR'AN 107:2	يَدُعُّ الْيَتِيمَ

There are twenty places in the Holy Qur'an where even a little carelessness in pronouncing a word can make one guilty of the unintended utterance of the words of blasphemy (كُفْرٌ).

The changing or transposing of ḥaraka (fatha, ḍamma, kasra) can alter the meanings of words and to intentionally read incorrectly can plunge one into the act of a major sin. The twenty places where one should exercise greatest care are as follows:

TABLE 11: TWENTY PLACES WHERE MISPRONUNCIATION CAN CHANGE THE MEANING

No.	VERSE NUMBER	SŪRA'S NAME	CORRECT READING	INCORRECT READING
1.	٤-١	اَلْفَاتِحَةُ	اِيَّاكَ نَعْبُدُ	اِيَاكَ نَعْبُدُ
2.	٧-١	اَلْفَاتِحَةُ	اَنْعَمْتَ عَلَيْهِمْ	اَنْعَمْتُ عَلَيْهِمْ
3.	١٢٤-٢	اَلْبَقَرَةُ	وَاِذِ ابْتَلٰى اِبْرٰهِيمَ رَبُّهُ	وَاِذِ ابْتَلٰى اِبْرٰهِيمُ رَبَّه
4.	٢٥١-٢	اَلْبَقَرَةُ	وَقَتَلَ دَاوُدُ جَالُوتَ	وَقَتَلَ دَاوُدَ جَالُوتَ
5.	٢٥٥-٢	اَلْبَقَرَةُ	اَللّٰهُ لَآ اِلٰهَ اِلَّا هُوَ	اَللّٰهُ لَآ اِلٰهَ اِلَّا هُوَ
6.	٢٦٢-٢	اَلْبَقَرَةُ	وَاللّٰهُ يُضَاعِفُ	وَاللّٰهُ يُضَاعَفُ
7.	١٦٥-٤	اَلنِّسَاءُ	رُسُلاً مُبَشِّرِينَ وَمُنْذِرِينَ	رُسُلاً مُبَشِّرِينَ وَمُنْذَرِينَ
8.	٣-٩	اَلتَّوْبَةُ	اَنَّ اللّٰهَ بَرِيٓءٌ مِنَ الْمُشْرِكِينَ وَرَسُولُهُ	اَنَّ اللّٰهَ بَرِيٓءٌ مِنَ الْمُشْرِكِينَ وَرَسُولِهِ
9.	١٥-١٧	بَنِي اِسْرَائِيلُ	وَمَا كُنَّا مُعَذِّبِينَ	وَمَا كُنَّا مُعَذَّبِينَ
10.	١٢١-٢٠	طٰهٰ	وَعَصٰى اٰدَمُ رَبَّهُ	وَعَصٰى اٰدَمَ رَبُّهُ
11.	٨٧-٢١	اَلْأَنْبِيَاءُ	اِنِّى كُنْتُ مِنَ الظَّالِمِينَ	اِنِّي كُنْتَ مِنَ الظَّالِمِينَ
12.	١٩٤-٢٦	اَلشُّعَرَاءُ	لِتَكُونَ مِنَ الْمُنْذِرِينَ	لِتَكُونَ مِنَ الْمُنْذَرِينَ
13.	٢٨-٣٥	فَاطِرُ	اِنَّمَا يَخْشَى اللّٰهَ مِنْ عِبَادِهِ الْعُلَمٰٓؤُا	اِنَّمَا يَخْشَى اللّٰهُ مِنْ عِبَادِهِ الْعُلَمٰٓؤُا
14.	٧٢-٣٧	اَلصَّافَّاتُ	وَلَقَدْ اَرْسَلْنَا فِيهِمْ مُنْذِرِينَ	وَلَقَدْ اَرْسَلْنَا فِيهِمْ مُنْذَرِينَ
15.	٢٤-٥٩	اَلْحَشْرُ	هُوَ اللّٰهُ الْخَالِقُ الْبَارِئُ الْمُصَوِّرُ	هُوَ اللّٰهُ الْخَالِقُ الْبَارِئُ الْمُصَوَّرُ
16.	٢٧-٤٨	اَلْفَتْحُ	صَدَقَ اللّٰهُ وَرَسُولُهُ	صَدَقَ اللّٰهَ رَسُولُهُ
17.	٣٧-٦٩	اَلْحَاقَّةُ	لَا يَاْكُلُهُ اِلَّا الْخَاطِئُونَ	لَا يَاْكُلُهُ اِلَّا الْخَاطَئُونَ

18.	١٦-٧٣	اَلْمُزَّمِّلُ	فَعَصَى فِرْعَوْنُ الرَّسُولَ	فَعَصَى فِرْعَوْنَ الرَّسُولُ
19.	٤١-٧٧	اَلْمُرْسَلَاتُ	فِي ظِلَالٍ وَعُيُونٍ	فِي ظَلَالٍ وَعُيُونٍ
20.	٤٥-٧٩	اَلنّٰزِعَاتُ	اِنَّمَا اَنْتَ مُنْذِرُ مَنْ يَخْشٰهَا	اِنَّمَآ اَنْتَ مُنْذَرُ مَنْ يَخْشٰهَا

CHAPTER SEVEN

MANNERS OF RECITATION

THE RULES OF QUR'ANIC RECITATION

اٰدَابُ التِّلَاوَةِ

For perfect recitation of the Qur'an, besides proper articulations of the letters according to the rules of Tajwīd , it is also important to know proper manners and to follow a number of objective and subjective conditions.

In his most famous work,[49] Al-Ghazali presented the recitation of the Qur'an in an elaborate, systematic, profound, and penetrating manner. He mentioned two sets of rules under the titles "External Rules" and "Mental Tasks." His belief that both external and mental tasks are important is in agreement with Islamic religious teaching on the subject. Those rules that are most readily applicable to the art of recitation are presented here in a summarized form.

OBJECTIVE CONDITIONS OF THE QUR'ANIC RECITATION

The following are the objective conditions for a perfect recitation of the Holy Qur'an.

1. CONDITION OF THE QUR'ANIC RECITER

The reciter of the Qur'an should be in a state of ablution (*wudu'*), either standing or sitting, facing the qibla with the head cast down, neither sitting crossed legged nor leaning against nor sitting in a haughty manner. He should sit as he would when sitting in front of his teacher.

According to Al-Ghazali, the best condition of the recitation is during the Prayer standing and inside a mosque. The Prophet said, "The parts of the land dearest to Allah are its mosques, and the parts most hateful to God are its markets." (Sahih Muslim)

Following the conditions above are the most excellent acts of the reciter. If, however, one recites the Qur'an without ablution while reclining on his side on a bed, he has also excellence, but this excellence is of a lower rank.

---

[49] Abu Hamid Muhammad al-Ghazali, *Ihya' 'Ulumi'd-Din* (The Revival of the Religious Sciences).

﴿الَّذِينَ يَذْكُرُونَ اللهَ قِيَامًا وَقُعُودًا وَعَلَى جُنُوبِهِمْ وَيَتَفَكَّرُونَ فِي خَلْقِ السَّمَاوَاتِ وَالْأَرْضِ﴾

[People of understanding are] those who remember God standing, sitting and lying on their sides, and ponder over the creation of the heavens and the Earth. (Āl 'Imrān 3:191)

Thus, Allah has praised all three conditions: He has, however, mentioned first the condition of standing in rememberance of Allah (ذِكْرٌ), then the condition of sitting and lastly the rememberance of Allah lying on one's side.

2. HOW MUCH TO RECITE

The best way to determining how much of the Qur'an one should read at a time is to rely upon the traditions of the Prophet, who said: "One who has read the [entire] Qur'an in fewer than three days has not understood it" (At-Tirmidhi, Abu Dawud, Ibn Maja).

This is because, according to Al-Ghazali, a swift reading prevents the reader from reading in a slow and distinct manner (following the *tartīl* اَلتَّرْتِيلُ).

The Prophet ordered 'Abd Allah ibn 'Umar to read the entire Qur'an once in every seven days. The Prophet's Companions 'Uthman ibn 'Affan, Zaid ibn Thabit, Ibn Masu'd, and Ubayy ibn Ka'b used to complete the reading of the entire Qur'an on every Friday.

3. SLOW AND DISTINCT MANNER (TARTĪL)

The recitation of the Qur'an in a slow and distinct manner (*Tartīl*) is commanded by Allah the Almighty:

﴿وَرَتِّلِ الْقُرْآنَ تَرْتِيلاً﴾

And recite the Qur'an in a slow and distinct manner. (al-Muzzammil 73:4)

The Prophet's wife Umm Salama described the Qur'an recitation of the Messenger, when she was asked about it: "Immediately [after being asked] she began to describe its recitation as clear and distinct in respect of every letter" (An-Nasai', at-Tirmidhi, Musnad Ibn Hanbal).

The reading of the Qur'an in a slow and distinct manner is praiseworthy (*mustahabb*), because it assists pondering (*tadabbur*) over it and reflection on its meaning (*tafakkur*). For a non-Arab who does not understand the meaning of the Qur'an, it is also praiseworthy to read it in a slow and distinct manner with pauses between the sentences because this is nearer to reverence and respect (which the Qur'an deserves) and stronger in its impression on the soul than babbling with haste.

'Abd Allah ibn 'Abbas said, "To read the Sūra al-Baqara and the Sūra Āl 'Imran in a slow and distinct manner while pondering over them, is better for me than to read the entire Qur'an babbling."

The Prophet said, "Adorn the Qur'an with your voices." (Sahih al-Bukhari, An-Nasai, Ibn Maja) He also said, "Allah does not listen to anything as much as He listens to man's sweet voice at the recitation of the Qur'an." (Sahih al-Bukhari, Sahih Muslim)

One night the Prophet listened to the recitation of Qur'an by 'Abd Allah ibn Mas'ud and with him were Abu Bakr and 'Uthman. They stood still for a long time [listening]. Then the Prophet said, "One who wants to read the Qur'an as fresh as it was revealed, should read it following the reading of Ibn Umm 'Abd." (Ibn Maja, Ibn Hanbal Musnad)

4. WEEPING DURING THE RECITATION

The Messenger of Allah commanded: "Recite the Qur'an and weep. If you do not weep naturally, then force yourself to weep." (Ibn Maja)

In the Qur'an, weeping is praised:

﴿وَيَخِرُّونَ لِلْأَذْقَانِ يَبْكُونَ وَيَزِيدُهُمْ خُشُوعًا﴾

They fall down on their faces in tears, and it increases their [earnest] humility. (Al-Isrā' 7:109)

Al-Ghazali said: "The method of forcing oneself to weep consists in bringing grief to the mind. If the eyes of anyone reciting the Qur'an do not weep, his mind should weep, i.e., be filled with grief and fear of God. The method of bringing grief to the mind of the Qur'an reader is through reflecting on the threats, warnings, covenants, and promises which are contained in the Qur'an. Then the reader will weep on his own shortcomings in respect of the commandments of the Qur'an and its threats of punishment. Thus, he will necessarily be aggrieved and will weep. The Qur'an reader should supplicate as: 'O Allah, make me one of those who weep for fear of You, and who are humble towards You.'"

5. RECITATIONAL PROSTRATION سَجْدَةُ التِّلاوَة

During the recitation of the Qur'an, if someone reads the verses of prostration, he should perform prostration سَجْدَةُ التِّلاوَة. Likewise, if someone hears a verse of prostration recited by another person, he himself should prostrate only if he is physically and ritually clean.[50]

According to the Hanafi School of Islamic Jurisprudence, there are fourteen verses of prostration in the Qur'an. However according to the Shafi'i and Hanbali Schools of jurisprudence, there are two verses of prostration in Sūra al-Hajj (22:18, and 22:77).

6. SUPPLICATIONS BEFORE, DURING, AND AFTER RECITATION

Before the recitation of the Qur'an, the reciter is commanded to seek refuge in Allah from Satan:

﴿فَإِذَا قَرَأْتَ الْقُرْآنَ فَاسْتَعِذْ بِاللهِ مِنَ الشَّيْطَانِ الرَّجِيمِ﴾

When you read the Qur'an, seek the protection of Allah from Satan, the Rejected One. (an-Nahl 16:98)

He should also supplicate:

﴿أَعُوذُ بِاللهِ السَّمِيعِ الْعَلِيمِ مِنَ الشَّيْطَانِ الرَّجِيمِ
رَبِّ أَعُوذُ بِكَ مِنْ هَمَزَاتِ الشَّيَاطِينِ ، وَأَعُوذُ بِكَ رَبِّ أَنْ يَحْضُرُونِ﴾

I seek the protection of Allah, the All-hearing, the All-knowing, against the rejected Satan. Lord; I seek refuge with You from the incitements of satans, and I seek refuge with You, Lord, lest they should approach me. (al-Mu'minūn 23:97)

He should also supplicate by reading the very last sūra of the Qur'an (an-Nās) and the Qur'an's opening sūra of al-Fatiha.

During the recitation of the Qur'an, on the verses of glorification of Allah, glorify Him and magnify Him. On the supplication and forgiveness of Allah, supplicate and seek forgiveness. On telling of any hopeful matter, pray to Allah for it. On a frightening matter, seek the protection of Allah from it. One can do these with his tongue or with his mind.

On completion of the Qur'an, the following prayer should be read:

---

50 See Recitational Prostration (later in this chapter) for a detail discussion on requirements of prostration, method of prostration, and supplication while prostrating.

God has spoken the truth,	صَدَقَ اللهُ الْعَظِيمُ
and His Messenger has conveyed	وَبَلَّغَ رَسُولُ اللهِ صَلَّى اللهُ
[it to us]	عَلَيْهِ وَسَلَّمَ
God, benefit us with the Qur'an;	اَللَّهُمَّ، اِنْفَعْنَا بِه
and bless us in it.	وَبَارِكْ لَنَا فِيهِ
Praise be to God,	اَلْحَمْدُ لِلّٰهِ
the Lord of the worlds!	رَبِّ الْعَالَمِينَ
I seek the forgiveness of God,	وَاسْتَغْفِرُ اللهَ
the Ever-Living, Self-subsisting and All-sustaining.	اَلْحَيَّ الْقَيُّومَ

7. LOUD RECITATION OF THE QUR'AN

There is no doubt that it is necessary to read the Qur'an loud enough so that the reader can hear it himself because recitation means distinguishing clearly between sounds.

As for reciting so loud that it can be heard by others, it is considered praise worthy in one respect and undesirable in another.

SILENT READING OF THE QUR'AN

With respect to the merits of reading the Qur'an silently, the Prophet said:

> The excellence of silent reading of the Qur'an compared with reading it aloud is like the excellence of secret almsgiving compared with public almsgiving. (Abu Dawud, an-Nasai, at-Tirmidhi, Musnad ibn Hanbal)

The Prophet also said:

> The best measure of sustenance (رِزْقٌ) is that which is sufficient, and the best mode of invocation of Allah (ذِكْرٌ) is that which is secret. (Musnad Ibn Hanbal)

The Prophet forbade reading the Qur'an loud in the following tradition:

> Some of you will not read the Qur'an aloud near others during the time between Maghrib (Sunset Prayer) and 'Isha (Night Prayer). (Musnad Ibn Hanbal)

LOUD READING OF THE QUR'AN

It is related that the Prophet once heard a group of his Companions reading the Qur'an aloud in the supererogatory Prayer performed after midnight (صَلٰوةُ الَّيلِ) and approved of this.

The Prophet said:

> If one of you keeps vigil at night performing supererogatory Prayer, he should read the Qur'an aloud, the angels as well as those who are staying at his house listen to this Qur'an-recitation and pray to Allah with his Prayer." (Sahih al-Bukhari, Sahih Muslim, Abu Dawud)

Once the Prophet passed by three of his Companions who were engaged in different modes of Qur'an-recitation. He passed by Abu Bakr who was reading the Qur'an silently. The Prophet asked him concerning the reason for this. He replied, "The One to Whom I am whispering can hear me." The Prophet passed by 'Uthman who was reading the Qur'an aloud. He asked him the reason for this. 'Uthman replied, "I am awakening those who are asleep and threatening the Satan." The Prophet passed by Bilal who was reading some verses from one sūra and other verses from another sūra. The Prophet asked him the reason. He replied, "I am mingling good things with other good things." The Prophet remarked, "Everyone of you has done good and right."

One may think that the above quoted traditions on aloud and silent reading are conflicting. However, this apparent confliction is that the silent reading of the Qur'an is far from ostentation رِيَاءٌ and affectation. Ostentation is an act to please man through a devotional act. It is strongly prohibited in the Qur'an (4:142, 107:6, 2:264, 4:38, 8:47), and in the Traditions it is called the lesser polytheism. (اَلشِّرْكُ الصَّغِيرُ) (Musnad ibn Hanbal).

All devotional acts must be performed only for Allah:

﴿فَمَنْ كَانَ يَرْجُوا لِقَآءَ رَبِّهِ فَلْيَعْمَلْ عَمَلاً صَالِحًا
وَلاَ يُشْرِكْ بِعِبَادَةِ رَبِّهِ اَحَدًا﴾

> Whoever expects to meet his Lord, let him work righteousness, and in the worship of his Lord admit no one as partner. (al-Kahf 18:110)

Therefore, for a reader who is afraid of ostentation and affectation, it is better to read the Qur'an silently.

In case one is not afraid of the act of ostentation and affectation, and if his loud recitation of the Qur'an does not disturb others, then recitation aloud is preferable for the following reasons:

- It involves more effort.
- Its benefit is also linked up with others (a good which involves other people is better than a good which does not).
- Loud recitation awakens the mind of the reader, unites his care for reflection on the (meanings of the verses of the) Qur'an and turns his ears to it.
- Loud recitation repels sleep.
- It adds to the energy for recitation and decreases the laziness.
- Waking a sleeping man can be expected from loud recitation.
- Sometimes, having seen the loud reader, an idle man with nothing to do gets energized and gets encouragement to serve Allah.

When one or more of the above intentions are present, the loud recitation of the Qur'an is better than silent reading.

MENTAL TASKS IN RECITATION

According to Imam al-Ghazali, there are ten mental tasks (or subjective conditions) in the recitation of the Qur'an.

1. UNDERSTANDING THE MAGNIFICATION OF THE DIVINE SPEECH

While reciting the Qur'an, the reader should consider the Qur'an and its elevated nature, the bounty of Allah, and His Kindness towards His creatures—humankind and jinn, descending from the throne of His Majesty to the level of their understanding.

2. MAGNIFICATION OF THE SPEAKER

The reciter should remember that he is not reading the speech of a human being. He should bring to his mind mangification of the One Who speaks in the Qur'an—Allah Almighty. Magnification of the Speaker will never come to the mind unless the reci-tor reflects of His Attributes, His Majesty and His Works. Thus, when the idea of the Supreme Divine Throne, of the heavens, of the Earth, and all in between them, jinn, man and other moving creatures and trees comes to the mind, he should know with certainty that the Creator of all these things is Allah who has no partners and He has absolute power over them. If He bestows favor upon them, then this is through His bounty, and if He punishes them, then this is by His Justice.

3. ATTENTION TO THE VERSES RECITED

The attribute of paying attention to the verses recited is generated from the preced-ing attribute which is the Magnification of the Speaker because a person who magnifies the speech of Allah can neither be inattentive to nor his thought be separated from what is being recited.

4. PONDERING OVER THE VERSES

This is more than the attention of the mind because sometimes a man who is reciting the Qur'an is not thinking and pondering over it. For this reason, it is a sunna act to recite the Qur'an in a slow and distinct manner (Qur'an 73:4).

'Ali ibn Abi Talib (the fourth caliph) said:

> There is no good in a devotional act which is not understood, nor in the recitation of the Qur'an which is not pondered over.

Pondering over verses can be strengthened by repeating them. It is related that the Prophet read, "بِسْمِ اللهِ الرَّحْمٰنِ الرَّحِيمِ" (In the name of God, the All-Merciful, the All-Compassionate) and repeated it twenty times. Certainly he repeated it in order to ponder over its meanings.

Abu Dharr related: "One night the Messenger of Allah kept vigil at night along with us. He kept vigil repeating a single verse which is:

﴿إِنْ تُعَذِّبْهُمْ فَإِنَّهُمْ عِبَادُكَ وَإِنْ تَغْفِرْ لَهُمْ فَإِنَّكَ
أَنْتَ الْعَزِيزُ الْحَكِيمُ﴾

> 'If You punish them they are Your servant, and if You forgive them, surely You are the Mighty, the Wise'" (al-Māedah 5:21). (An-Nasa'i, Ibn Maja)

5. UNDERSTANDING THE MEANING

The Qur'an encompasses the discussion of the Attributes of Allah, the discussion of His works, the discussion of the circumstances of those who considered them false and how they were destroyed, the description of Allah's commandments and threats, the description of Paradise and Hell and so on.

The Qur'an-reciter should reflect[51] on the meanings of Allah's Names and Attributes so that deep connotations[52] may be disclosed to him.

As for the works of Allah, the Qur'an-reciter should understand from them the Attributes of Allah, since the existence of a work proves the existence of the Doer, or Agent, and the greatness of the former proves the greatness of the latter. One who

---

[51] To think quietly and calmly.

[52] The significance of something; to convey in addition to exact explicit meaning.

knows the True One sees Him in everything since everything orginates from Him, returns to Him, subsists on Him, and belongs to Him.

As for the hardship faced by the Prophets, when the Qur'an-reciter hears how they were considered false, persecuted, and some of them were even killed, he should understand from this the Divine Attribute of independence from His Messengers and from those to whom they were sent, and that if He destroys all of them this will not affect anything in His kingdom. When he hears of God's help to the Messengers in the end, he should understand the Power of God and His Will to further the truth.

As for the circumstances of the deniers of God, e.g., the people of 'Ad and the people of Thamud, and the evil that happened to them, the reader's understanding of these should result in a feeling of fear of God's assault and His revenge.

When the reader hears the description of Paradise and Hell and other things in the Qur'an, such as promises and threats, hope and fear, he should try to understand the proper meaning in each case.

6. GETTING RID OF ALL OBSTACLES

Most people are hindered from understanding the meanings of the Qur'an. There are a number of reasons for this:

a. Reciting the Qur'an for mere show to others causes one to divert his attention from understanding the meanings;

b. The reciter is a strict follower مُقَلِّد of a particular School of thought مَذْهَب and he follows or imitates what he has heard, without arriving at it by spiritual insight and mystic vision مُشَاهَدَة.

c. One's insistence upon sin, or his being characterized by pride, or his being afflicted with worldly passion which he runs after prevents him from benefitting fully from the Qur'an. When worldly desires greatly accumulate within the soul, the meanings of Divine Speech are greatly veiled. When worldly burdens on the soul are made light, reflection on its meaning become clear.

d. The fourth obstacle in understanding the meaning of the Qur'an is present when someone has read the outward exegesis[53] (*tafsir* تَفْسِير) of the Qur'an and has formed the belief that Qur'anic verses have only those meanings which have come down by traditions from Ibn 'Abbas, Mujahid, etc., and that meanings going beyond them are interpretation of the Qur'an by personal

[53] An explanation or critical interpretation of a text.

opinion and that 'he who has explained the Qur'an by his personal opinion, has taken his place in Hell!'[54]

7. THE TEACHING OF THE QUR'AN

The reciter should bear in mind that every part of the Qur'an is intended for him. If he reads any command in the Qur'an, he will suppose that he is the one commanded. If he comes across any prohibition contained in a Qur'anic verse, he will suppose he is the one to whom the prohibition applies. Likewise, if he learns any promise of reward or any punishment, he will make the same assumption.

If he reads the stories of the bygone nations and the Prophets, he will know that they are not intended for chatting but they should be considered to derive a lesson. The Qur'an-reciter should suppose that God has made His mind firm by narrating in it the stories of Prophets, their patience while suffering, and their steadfastness in religion while waiting for help from God.

8. FEEL THE QUR'AN

What this means is that the mind of the reciter will be affected by different feelings according to the different verses recited. Thus, he will be in a state of grief, fear, hope, and so on.

Thus, when reading a verse which warns or restricts the Divine forgiveness to those who fulfill certain stipulations, he will make himself so small as if he is about to die out of fear. When a verse about the promise of forgiveness is recited, he will rejoice as if he flies for joy. When Allah, His Attributes and Names are mentioned, he will bow his head in submission to His Majesty and in acknowledgement of His greatness. When he reads a verse on some nonbelievers' faith in an impossible thing for Allah (such as Allah has a child and a consort), he will lower his voice and be broken-hearted because of the evil of what they have believed. When Paradise is described, he will produce in his mind a yearning for it; but when Hell is described he will tremble for fear of it.

9. HEARING THE SPEECH OF ALLAH

The Qur'an-reciter gradually rises to the state in which he feels that he is hearing the Speech of Allah from Allah and not from himself.

According to Al-Ghazali, there are three levels of the recitation of the Qur'an:

---

[54] Al-Ghazali, in his defence of sufistic interpretation of the Qur'an, devoted the fourth chapter of his work to this topic in *Ihya' 'Ulumi'd-Din* (The Revival of the Religious Sciences).

a. The first rank is attained when a man supposes that he is reading the Qur'an to Allah, standing in front of Him, and He is looking at him and listening to what is being recited,
b. The second rank is attained when a man views with his mind that Allah is seeing him, addressing him with His kindness, and secretly conversing with him with His gifts and beneficence,
c. The last rank is attained when a man feels that he is seeing the Speaker (i.e. Allah) in the Speech (i.e. Qur'an) and His Attributes in its sentences.

The first and second are the spiritual ranks of 'the people on the right' (اَصْحَابُ الْيَمِينِ).

The third one is the highest grade of those 'drawn near to Allah' (اَلْمُقَرَّبُونَ).

All other grades form the grades of those who are 'inattentive people' (اَلْغَافِلُونَ).

10. GETTING RID OF FALSE SATISFACTION

When the Qur'an-reader recites verses on promise to, and praise of the pious, he will not view himself as one of them; rather he will view those who have the most certain faith and those are the most truthful in religion and will hope that Allah will join him with them. When he recites verses on Divine dislike and Divine reproach of the disobedient and those falling short of duties commanded by Allah, he will suppose that he is the one addressed and intended in these verses.

THE RECITATIONAL PROSTRATIONS

سُجُودُ التِّلَاوَةِ

Anyone who recites a verse of prostration, or hears its recital, is required to perform a *sajda* (prostration) so that one's physical state may be in agreement with the angels near to Allah to give a practical proof of one's humility, servitude, and obedience to Allah simultaneously with His angels.

The Arabic phrase يُسَبِّحُونَهُ (*yusab-biḥūna-hū*) means: "They acknowledge and declare that 'Allah is flawless and is absolutely free from every sort of defect, error or weakness, and He neither has any partners nor is there anyone like Him,' and that they are always engaged in this."

TABLE 12 : THE RECITATIONAL PROSTRATIONS

SEQ. NO.	SŪRA NO	SŪRA NAME / VERSE NO	JUZ	HIZB	CAUSE OF THE PROSTRATION اَلْموجِبُ السَّجْدَةِ	SUBJECT OF THE PROSTRATION اَلْموضُوعُ السَّجْدَةِ
1.	7	AL-A'RĀF: 206	9	24	Bow down before Him يَسْجُدُونَ	Bow down before Him يَسْجُدُونَ
2.	13	AR-RA'D: 15	13	2	Prostrate themselves to God وَلِلّٰهِ يَسْجُدُ	And the evening وَالْاٰصَالِ
3.	16	AN-NAHL: 49-50	14	6	And prostrate to God وَلِلّٰهِ يَسْجُدُ	They are commanded مَا يُؤْمَرُونَ
4.	17	AL-ISRĀ': 109	15	12	Fall down on their faces in humble prostration يَخِرُّونَ لِلْاَذْقَانِ	Humility خُشُوعًا
5.	19	MARYAM: 58	16	4	They fall down in prostrate adoration خَرُّوا سُجَّدًا	Weeping (in tears) بُكِيًّا
6.	22	AL-HAJJ: 18	17	2	Bow down in adoration يَسْجُدُ لَهُ	All that He wills مَا يَشَاۤءُ

7.	22	AL-HAJJ: 77 (Imam Shafi'i only)	17	10	Prostrate yourself وَاسْجُدُوا	You may prosper تُفْلِحُونَ
8.	25	AL-FURQĀN: 60	19	5	Adore اُسْجُدُوا	Flight [from the truth] نُفُورًا
9.	27	AN-NAML: 25-26	19	2	That they worship not God اَلاَّ يَسْجُدُوا لِلّٰهِ	The Lord of the throne supreme رَبِّ الْعَرْشِ الْعَظِيمِ
10.	32	AS-SAJDA: 15	21	2	Fall down in prostrate خَرُّوا سُجَّدًا	Not puffed up with pride لَا يَسْتَكْبِرُونَ
11.	38	SĀD: 24 (Imam Abu Hanifa and Imam Malik)	23	2	And he bowed himself and fell down prostrate وَخَرَّ رَاكِعًا	And repented وَاَنَابَ
12.	41	FUSSILĀT: 37-38 (All except Imam Malik)	24	5	And adore God وَاسْجُدُوا لِلّٰهِ	They never tire (are fed up) لَا يَسْئَمُونَ
13.	53	AN-NAJM: 62 (All except Imam Malik)	26	3	Prostrate yourself فَاسْجُدُوا	And Serve Him وَاعْبُدُوا
14.	84	AL-INSHIQĀQ: 21 (All except Imam Malik)	30	1	Fall Prostrate يَسْجُدُونَ	Fall Prostrate يَسْجُدُونَ
15.	96	AL-'ALAQ: 19 (All except Imam Malik)	30	1	Bow down in prostration وَاسْجُدْ	And bring thyself close وَاقْتَرِبْ

According to the Hanafi School of jurisprudence, there are fourteen verses[55] of the Holy Qur'an, the recital of which requires the performance of a prostration. Though all the jurists (فقهاء) agree that a prostration should be performed at these places, there is a difference in regard to its obligatory status. According to Imam Abu Hanifa, it is compulsory (وَاجِبٌ) but the other scholars are of the opinion that it is optional (نَفْلٌ) or sunna (سُنَّةٌ). It may also be noted that a thing which is sunna is not as binding as wājib but its intentional omission, though not sinful, is considered bad for a true Muslim and its permanent abandonment is sinful.

A complete list of all Recitational Prostration is given in Table 12 above.

HOW TO PERFORM THE SAJDA

As regard to the manner of performaning the recitational sajda, we learn from the traditions (اَحَادِيث) that it was different in form on different occasions. Sometimes,

55 See Table 12 for exact number of recitational prostrations according to each school of thought.

while the Noble Prophet was reciting a verse that required the performance of a sajda, he himself would prostrate then and there, and everyone in the gathering did the same, so much so that if one did not find room for it on the ground, he would perform it by laying his head on the back of the man in front of him. We also learn from the traditions that on the occasion of the conquest of Makka, when the Holy Prophet was reciting the Qur'an, a verse requiring the performance of sajda occured, then those who were standing performed it on the ground, while those who were riding their horses or camels performed it on the back of the animals they were riding. At times when the Prophet recited a verse requiring sajda during his address, he came down from the pulpit, and performed it on the ground and then climbed the pulpit and resumed his address.

THE CONDITIONS FOR THE PERFORMANCE OF THE SAJDA

The majority of Muslims are of the opinion that the conditions for the performance of the prostration of recitation are the same with the ones in the performance of the Prayer (صَلٰوة). But there is no proof for these conditions in the traditions of the Prophet concerning recitational sajda. We find from the traditions that when a person hears a verse requiring sajda, he should bend down his head (without raising his hands up to the ears for *takbir*) whenever and whatever position he may be, irrespective of these conditions. He should not mind whether he is in a state of ablution (وُضوء) or not; whether he can turn his face towards the qibla or not; whether it is possible for him to prostrate his head on the ground or not.

We find examples of the learned and pious Muslims in the past following the above practice. According to Imam al-Bukhari, 'Abdullah ibn 'Umar would perform sajda whether he was in a state of ablution or not. It is cited in *Fathu'l-Bari* that Abu 'Abdur Rahman Sulami would recite the Qur'an while he was walking and would merely bend down his head when he read a verse requiring sajda, whether he was in a state of ablution or not and whether he was facing the qibla or not.

Al-Ghazali presented the following in his *Ihya' 'Ulumi'd-Din* (The Revival of the Religious Sciences) regarding the performance of recitational sajda:

> The minimum requirement of prostration is that one prostrates by putting his forehead on the ground, [without uttering Allahu Akbar and without any supplication]. Its perfect form is for him to utter Allahu Akbar and then prostrate himself and, while prostrated, supplicate with that supplication which is appropriate to the verse of prostration recited. For example, if he has read the Words of God (Exalted is He):

﴿إِنَّمَا يُؤْمِنُ بِآيَاتِنَا الَّذِينَ إِذَا ذُكِّرُوا بِهَا خَرُّوا سُجَّدًا وَسَبَّحُوا بِحَمْدِ رَبِّهِمْ وَهُمْ لَا يَسْتَكْبِرُونَ﴾

Only those believe in Our signs, who, when they are reminded of them, fall down prostrate and celebrate the praises of their Lord and are not [ever] puffed up with pride. (as-Sajdah 32:15)

He will supplicate:

اَللّٰهُمَّ اجْعَلْنِي مِنَ السَّاجِدِينَ لِوَجْهِكَ وَالْمُسَبِّحِينَ بِحَمْدِكَ،
وَاَعُوذُ بِكَ اَنْ اَكُونَ مِنَ الْمُسْتَكْبِرِينَ عَنْ اَمْرِكَ، اَوْ عَلَى اَوْلِيَائِكَ

O God, make me one of those who prostrate themselves before You for Your pleasure and who glorify You with Your praise. I seek Your protection from being one of those who are arrogant against Your command or against Your friends.

On reading the Words of God (Exalted is He),

﴿وَيَخِرُّونَ لِلْاَذْقَانِ يَبْكُونَ وَيَزِيدُهُمْ خُشُوعًا﴾

"They weep while they prostrate themselves, and this adds to their humility." (al-Isrā' 17:109)

The Qur'an reciter will supplicate:

اَللّٰهُمَّ اجْعَلْنِي مِنَ الْبَاكِينَ اِلَيْكَ وَخَاشِعِينَ لَكَ

O God, make me one of those who weep for fear of You, and who are humble towards You.

Al-Ghazali further said:

It is necessary to fulfill those stipulations which are meant for ritual prayers (شُرُوطُ الصَّلوة), such as covering one's private parts (سَتْرُ الْعَوْرَة), facing the qibla and cleanliness of clothing and body against ritual impurity (*hadath*) and physical filth. A man who is not clean when hearing the verses of prostration will prostrate when he becomes clean.

It is said, in the perfect form of prostration due to Qur'an reading, the prostrater will utter Allahu Akbar, lifting his hands, thereby making all other things unlawful to himself. Then he will again utter Allahu Akbar while inclining towards prostration, [then he will prostrate]. Then he will utter Allahu Akbar while lifting the head [from prostration], and then he will make the salutation [turning face to the right and to the left]. Some authorities have added to this the reading of at-tashahhud. There is no basis for these views except an analogy (*qiyas*) with the prostration of ritual Prayer. This analogy, however, is far from being sound, because what has occured in the Qur'an is only the command of prostration, and so this command should be obeyed. The utterence of Allahu Akbar while inclining towards prostration is nearer to the beginning [and so this should be done]; all other things are far from what can be supported by Islamic jurisprudence.

We conclude from the above discussion that though the method followed by the majority is more prudent, if a person follows a practice different from that of the majority, he should not be reproved or criticized for this, because there is no proof in the traditions or sunnah for the method followed by the majority. One can recite the following verse at all times after performing the recitational sajda:

﴿سَمِعْنَا وَأَطَعْنَا غُفْرَانَكَ رَبَّنَا وَإِلَيْكَ الْمَصِيرُ﴾

We have heard [the call to faith and right conduct] and obeyed. Our Lord, grant us Your forgiveness, and to You is the homecoming. (al-Baqara 2:285)

THE SUPPLICATIONS

دُعَاءٌ

Upon a complete recitation of the entire Qur'an, a supplication (دُعَاءٌ) should be offered asking for Allah's forgiveness, mercy, light, and guidance.

Zain al-'Abidin, the son of Imam Husain, used to offer a supplication after a reading of the Qur'an (*Khatm al-Qur'an*). He prayed to Allah that the Qur'an be made his companion and guidance against the Satan and his evil suggestions, and that through the Qur'an his heart be purified to understand its wonders and to reject evil by the force of its maxims.

As-Suyuti has been quoted as recommending the following supplication for Divine assistance in committing the Qur'an to memory:

> I seek Thee O God, O Most Gracious, by Thy Majesty and the Light of Thy Countenance, to bind to my heart the memorization of Thy Book as Thou hast taught me and endow me with [the capacity] to recite it with the grammatical inflection that shall cause Thee to be pleased with me. And I ask Thee O God, O Most Gracious, by Thy Majesty and the Light of Thy Countenance to illuminate my vision by means of Thy Book and to make my tongue fluent, and open my heart and dilate my breast and wash my body by its means. Indeed none but Thyself giveth it. And there is no strength nor power except in God, the Exalted, the Majestic.

The supplication after a complete recitation of the Qur'an is mostly added to the end of the *mushafs*. People can read or recite the supplication alone or together in congregation. There are varying *khatm* supplications; one can read any of these prayers and then supplicate to Allah. The following supplication in Arabic is one of those prayers recited upon completing the recitation of the entire Qur'an:

"O Allah! Change my fear in my grave into love:	اَللّٰهُمَّ آنِسْ وَحْشَتِي فِي قَبْرِي
O Allah! Have mercy on me in the name of the Great Qur'an;	اَللّٰهُمَّ ارْحَمْنِي بِالْقُرْآنِ الْعَظِيمِ

And make it for me a Leader [who leads to the truth] and Light and Guidance and Mercy;	وَاجْعَلْهُ لِي اِمَامًا وَنُورًا وَهُدًى وَرَحْمَةً
O Allah! Make me remember of what of it I have forgotten;	اَللّٰهُمَّ ذَكِّرْنِي مِنْهُ مَا نَسِيتُ
Make me know of it that which I have become ignorant of;	وَعَلِّمْنِي مِنْهُ مَا جَهِلْتُ
And make me recite it in the hours of the night and the day;	وَارْزُقْنِي تِلاَوَتَهُ اٰنَآءَ اللَّيْلِ وَاٰنَاءَ النَّهَارِ
And make it an argument for me O Thou Sustainer of [all] the worlds!	وَاجْعَلْهُ لِي حُجَّةً يَارَبَّ الْعَالَمِينَ
Āmīn!	آمِينَ

Appendices

APPENDIX A

The Glossary of the Arabic Words

'ABDULLAH BIN 'ABBAS	عَبْدُ اللهِ بِنْ عَبَّاس	A cousin and a great Companion of the Prophet.
'ABDULLAH BIN 'UMAR	عَبْدُ اللهِ بِنْ عُمَرْ	A Companion of the Prophet.
'ABDULLAH BIN MAS'UD	عَبْدُ اللهِ بِنْ مَسْعُود	A famous Companion of the Prophet and a great narrator of Traditions, an authority on the recitation of the Qur'an, its explanation (tafsir) and on legal matters. He was held in high esteem for his shrewdness, learning, integrity, dedication, and sincerety.
'ABDULLAH BIN 'AMR BIN AL-'AS	عَبْدُ اللهِ بِن عَمْرُو بِنِ الْعَاص	A Companion of the Prophet.
ABU 'ABDURRAHMAN SALAMI	أَبو عَبْدُ الرَّحْمٰنِ السَّلاَمِيّ	A Companion of the Prophet.
ABU BAKR AS-SIDDIQ	أَبو بَكْرِ الصِّدّيق	The first adult male person to accept Islam, father-in- law of the Prophet, his greatest Companion and the first Rightly-Guided Caliph of Islam.
ABU HANIFA	أَبو حَنِيفَة	Founder of the Hanafi School of Thought (jurisprudence).
AHĀDITH	اَحَادِيث	Plural of Hadith: the traditions of the Prophet.
AHKĀM	اَحْكَام	The Rules.
AL-BUKHARI	اَلْبُخَارِي	Muhammad bin Ismail al-Bukhari, who collected the most reliable Traditions of the Prophet in *Sahih Al-Bukhari*.
AL-BUKHARI, SAHIH	اَلْبُخَارِي، صَحِيح	The most reliable collection of the traditions of the Prophet.

AL-GHĀFILŪN	اَلْغَافِلُونَ	Inattentive people; those who neglect.
AL-GHAZALI	اَلْغَزَالِي	Abu Hamid Muhammad al-Ghazali, a Sufi and a great religious authority of Islam.
AL-MUQARRABŪN	اَلْمُقَرَّبُونَ	Those drawn near to God.
'ALI BIN ABI TALIB	عَلِي بِنِ اَبِي طَالِب	A cousin and son-in-law of the Prophet and the fourth Rightly-Guided Caliph of Islam.
ALIF MAQSŪRA	اَلِف مَقْصُورَة	Vertical alif; an alternate written form of alif.
AMIR MU'AWIA	اَمِيرُ مُعَاوِيَة	The fifth head of the Islamic State.
'AMR BIN AL-'AS	عَمْرُو بِن الْعَاص	A Companion of the Prophet.
'ARIḌ	عَارِض	Temporary
ASHABU'L-YAMIN	اَصْحَابُ الْيَمِين	The people on the right; Successful people.
'ASHRATA QIRĀ'AT	عَشَرَة قِرَاءَات	Ten recognized versions of the recitation of the Qur'an.
AT-TASHAH-HUD	اَلتَّشَهُّد	The recitation of the invocation "At-tahiyyatu lillahi" upto "wa-ashhadu anna Muhammadan Abduhu wa Rasuluhu" while in sitting posture in Prayer.
ĀYAH	آيَة	A verse of the Qur'an.
ĀYĀT	آيَات	Plural of Ayah; verses of the Qur'an.
BADAL	بَدَل	Substitution; change.
BASMALAH	بَسْمَلَة	Refers to: بِسْمِ اللهِ الرَّحمنِ الرَّحِيمِ "In the Name of Allah, the All-Merciful, All-Compassionate."
BILAL	بِلاَل	A Companion of the Prophet.
ḌAMMA	ضَمَّةْ	A vowel sign: ـُ
DHIKR	ذِكْر	An invocation of God; remembrance of God by glorifying Him.
DUĀ'	دُعَآء	Supplication; prayer.

FARD	فَرض	Obligatory.
FATHA	فَتْحَة	A vowel sign: ـَـ
FUQAHA’	فُقَهَاء	Islamic jurists; experts in Islamic jurisprudence.
GHUNNA	غُنَّة	Nasalization; Nasal sound.
HADITH	حَديث	A Tradition of the Prophet.
HADR	حَدر	A fast method of recitation of the Qur’an.
HAFIZ	حَافِظ	One who has memorized the entire Qur’an.
HAMZATU’L-WAṢL	هَمْزَةُ الوَصْل	See Waṣl, Hamzatu’l.
ḤARAKA	حَرَكَة	A vowel sign: Fatha, Ḍamma, Kasra.
HARFĪ	حَرْفِي	Referring to a letter.
HURŪF	حُرُوف	Plural of Harf: letters.
IBN HAZM	اِبن حَزْم	The Islamic scholar of the fifth century of the Hijra.
IBTIDA’	اِبْتِدَاء	Starting recitation of the Qur’an after a stop.
IDGHĀM	اِدْغَام	Merger; assimilation of one letter into another.
IDGHĀM, NĀQIS	اِدغَامٌ نَاقِص	A partial merger of nūn sakīn or tanwīn into another letter.
IDGHĀM, SHAFAWI	اِدغَامٌ شَفَوي	Labial merger; occurs in mīm sākin, if followed by a mushaddad
IDGHĀM, TĀMM	اِدغَامٌ تَام	A complete merger of nūn sakīn or tanwīn into the following letter under certain conditions.
IKHFĀ	اِخْفَاء	A slight nasal sound.
IKHFĀ, SḤAFAWĪ	اِخْفَاءٌ شَفَوي	A light nasalization in pronouncing mīm sākin if followed by bā ب .
IKHTILAS	اِختِلَاص	Slighting; lacking in strength; disregarding.
IMĀLA	اِمَالَة	To change fatha with Kasra. As in the word مَجرِيهَا (pronounced as Maj-ray-ha)

IQLĀB	اِقْلاَب	If the letter bā ب comes after nūn sakīn or tanwīn then nūn sakīn or tanwīn is changed into mīm.
ISKĀN	اِسْكَان	omitting vowels
ISTI'LĀ	اِسْتِعْلاَء	Refers to the letters kha خ, ṣād ص, ḍād ض, ṭā ط, ẓā ظ, ghain غ, and qāf ق, which are pronounced elevated (high).
IZHĀR	اِظْهَار	A clear and sharp pronunciation of a letter; usually refers to nūn sakīn, tanwīn, or mīm sākin without nasalization or lengthening مَدّ.
IZHĀR , SHAFAWĪ	اِظْهَارٌ شَفَوِي	A clear and sharp pronunciation of mīm sākin if followed by any letter except bā ب or mīm م.
JUZ	جُزْء	1/30 part of the Qur'an.
KALIMĪ	كَلِمِي	Referring to a word.
KASRA	كَسْرَة	A vowel sign: ـِ
KĀTIB	كَاتِب	A scribe; an official writer; specially refers to those Companions of the Prophet who wrote down the fragments of the Qur'an as dictated by the Prophet.
KHUBTH	خُبْث	Filth; ritual impurity.
KHALID BIN WALID	خَالِد بِن وَلِيد	A Companion of the Prophet and a well known General of the Islamic Armies.
LAHN, AL-JALĪ	لَحْنُ الْجَلِي	Clear errors in the recitation of the Qur'an.
LAHN, AL-KHAFĪ	لَحْنُ الْخَفِي	Minor errors in the recitation of the Qur'an.
LAYL	لَيْل	Night.
LĀM AL-FI'L	لاَمُ الفِعْل	The letter lām in verbs.
LĀM AL-JALĀLAH	لاَمُ الْجَلاَلَة	The letter lām in the word Allah ﷲ or Allahumma اَللَّهُمَّ.

LĀM AL-QAMARIYYA	لَامُ الْقَمَرِيَّة	The lām of the adjectives or nouns which is not assimilated (merged), e.g.: Al-Qamar اَلْقَمَر Al-Qalam اَلْقَلَم .
LĀM AT-TA'RĪF	لَامُ التَّعْرِيف	The definite article (particular nouns) is indicated by Al اَل in Arabic, e.g.: Al-Qamar اَلْقَمَر .
LĀM ASH-SHAMSIYYA	لَامُ الشَّمْسِيَّة	When lām of the adjectives or nouns is assimilated (merged), it is known as lām Ash-Shamsiyya, e.g. ash-Shams اَلشَّمس , ad-Dunya اَلدُّنيَا .
LĪN LETTERS	حُرُوفُ اللِّين	The two letters waw and alif when sākin and preceded by a fatha are known as Līn letters; they are pronounced softly.
MADD	مَدّ	The lengthening of letters alif, waw or yā in pronunciation.
MADD 'ĀRIḌ	مَدٌّ عَارِض	A temporary Madd; it occurs due to temporary Sukūn when waqf is made.
MADD 'ĀRIḌ LĪN	مَدٌّ عَارِضٌ لِين	A Temporary Soft Madd.
MADD ASLĪ	مَدٌّ اَصْلِي	A real Madd when the letters of Madd are not followed by a Sukūn, Shadda, or hamza.
MADD FARA'Ī	مَدٌّ فَرْعِي	A derived Madd when the letters of Madd are followed by a Sukūn, Shadda, or hamza.
MADD HARFĪ	مَدٌّ حَرْفِي	A type of Derived Madd which is caused by a real sukūn or tashdīd in a letter.
MADD JĀ'IZ	مَدٌّ جَائِز	Also known as Madd al-Munfaṣil; the letter of Madd a permanent Sukūn or Shadda.
MADD KALIMĪ	مَدٌّ كَلِمِي	A type of Derived Madd which is caused by a real sukūn or tashdīd in a word.
MADD LĀZIM	مَدٌّ لَازِم	A type of Derived Madd caused by a permanent Sukūn.
MADD MUTTAṢIL	مَدٌّ مُتَّصِل	A type of Derived Madd caused by a hamza in the same word, also known as Madd al-Muttaṣil (Compulsory Madd).

MADD ṢILAH	مَدٌّ صِلَة	A type of Derived Madd in which Condition of Madd and Cause of Madd are in two consecutive words; the condition of Madd is written as (ـهِ ، هِ ، ـهُ ، هُ).
MADD TABI'Ī	مَدٌّ طَبِيعِي	A real Madd; also known as Madd Asli.
MADD TALAFFUẒĪ	مَدٌّ تَلَفُّظِي	Same as Madd Ṣilah.
MADD WĀJIB	مَدٌّ وَاجِب	A type of Derived Madd in which Cause of Madd is hamza and it is in the same word.
MADD WAQFĪ	مَدٌّ وَقْفِي	Same as Temporary Madd.
MADHHAB	مَذْهَب	A school of thought, e.g.: Hanafi, Shafi'i, Hanbali, or Maliki.
MADHHAB, HANAFĪ	مَذْهَبٌ حَنَفِي	The school of thought named after Imam Abu Hanifa.
MADHHAB, HANBALĪ	مَذْهَبٌ حَنْبَلِي	The school of thought named after Imam Hanbal.
MADHHAB, MALIKĪ	مَذْهَبٌ مَالِكِي	The school of thought named after Imam Malik.
MADHHAB, SHAFI'Ī	مَذْهَبٌ شَافِعِي	The school of thought named after Imam Shafi'i.
MAKHĀRIJ	مَخَارِج	Plural of Makhraj: The places of articulation.
MAKHRAJ	مَخْرَج	A place of articulation.
MU'ĀNAQA	مُعَانَقَة	A term used in the recitation of the Qur'an where a certain word or phrase is enclosed by three dots; one may stop at either the first or the second occurrence of three dots but not at both.
MUKHAFFAF	مُخَفَّف	A letter with sukūn.
MUQALLID	مُقَلِّد	A follower of a particular school of thought (jurisprudence); e.g. Hanifī, Malikī, Sha'faī, or Hanbalī.
MUQATTA'ĀT	مُقَطَّعَات	Abbreviated letters prefixed before certain sūras, e.g. Alif-Lām-Mīm.
MURĀQABA	مُرَاقَبَة	Same as Mu'ānaqa.

MUSHADDAD	مُشَدَّد	A letter with Tashdīd.
MUSHAF	مُصْحَف	A scripture; applied to a copy of the Qur'an.
MUSHAHADA	مُشَاهَدَة	Mystic vision; observation.
MUSLIM, SAHIH	مُسْلِم، صَحِيح	A collection of the Traditions of the Prophet prepared by Imam Muslim.
MUSNAD, IBN HANBAL	مُسْنَد ابْن حَنْبَل	A collection of the traditions of the Prophet prepared by Imam Ibn Hanbal.
MUTA'KHKHIRĪN	مُتَأَخِّرِين	A term referring to later commentators of the Qur'an.
MUTAḤARRIK	مُتَحَرِّك	A letter with a vowel.
MUTAQADDIMĪN	مُتَقَدِّمِينَ	A term referring to Earlier Commentators of the Qur'an.
MUTHAQQAL	مُثَقَّل	A letter with tashdīd; same as Mushaddad.
NAFL	نَفْل	Optional.
NISF	نِصْف	One half (1/2).
NŪN QUTNI	نُونٌ قُطْنِي	A small nūn which is used to connect two words when the first word ends on tanwīn and the second word begins with a sākin letter.
RIYĀ' / OSTENTATION	اَلرِّيَاء	The desire to please men through a devotional act, it is strongly prohibited in the Qur'an: (2:264, 4:38, 4:142, 8:47, 107:6).
QALQALA	قَلْقَلَة	The echoing quality found in the letters qāf ق , ṭā ط , bā ب , jīm ج , and dāl د .
QĀRĪ	قَارِي	An expert in the recitation of the Qur'an.
QASR	قَصْر	Shortening.
QIBLA	قِبْلَة	The direction of the Holy Mosque, Ka'ba, in Makka.
QIYĀS	قِيَاس	An analogy.
RA'AL-MAWQUF	رَاءُ الْمَوقُوف	A sākin rā due to a waqf on it.

RAUM	رَوم	A type of waqf in which the sound of kasra or ḍamma is pronounced weak (about 1/3 of its original sound) to show that the letter on which waqf was made had kasra or ḍamma.
RIYA'	اَلرِّيَاء	Ostentation; show off; an act to gain merely worldly fame.
RIZQ	رِزق	Sustenance; everything needed by human beings to support life.
HIZB or RUBA'	رُبَع	One fourth (1/4).
RUKŪ'	رُكُوع	A part (or section) of a sūra consisting of a number of verses, a term used in India, Pakistan, and Bangladesh to indicate a portion of the Sūra.
SAHIH AL-BUKHARI	صَحِيحُ الْبُخَارِي	The most reliable collection of the Tradition of the Prophet prepared by Imam al-Bukhari.
SAHIH MUSLIM	صَحِيحُ مُسْلِم	The second most reliable collection of the traditions of the Prophet by Imam Muslim.
SAJDATU'T-TILĀWAH	سَجْدَةُ التِّلاوَة	A recitational prostration.
SĀKIN	سَاكِن	An absence of a vowel sign on a letter indicated by (ـْـ).
SAKTA	سَكْتَة	A pause without breaking breath.
SALĀTU'L-LAYL	صَلٰوةُ الَّيل	An optional Prayer performed after midnight and before Dawn Prayer.
SATRU'L-'AWRA	سَتْرَ الْعَوْرَة	Covering the private parts of the body.
SHADDA	شَدَّة	A sign (ـّـ) placed over a letter indicating its double pronunciation.
SHURUT AS-SALAH	شُرُوط الصَّلٰوة	Required conditions for offering Prayers.
SIFĀT	صِفَات	Quality of a letter with which it is pronounced.
SIPARA	سِيَارَه	1/30 of the Qur'an: also known as Para or Juz, used in India, Pakistan, etc.

SAB'A QIRĀ'AT	سَبعَة قِرَاءَات	Seven recognized versions of the recitation of the Qur'an.
SUKŪN	سُكُون	The symbol (ـْـ) indicating an absence of a vowel (ḥaraka) on a letter.
SUKŪN 'ĀRIḌ	سُكُونٌ عَارِض	A temporary sukūn due to stopping (waqf).
SUKŪN 'ASLĪ	سُكُونٌ اَصْلِي	A permanent sukūn which is retained in continuous reading (اَلْوَصْل) as well as in stopping (اَلْوَقْفُ).
SUNAN, ABU DAWUD	سُنَن اَبُو دَاود	A collection of the traditions of the Prophet by Imam Abu Dawud.
SUNAN, AD-DARIMI	سُنَنُ الدَّارِمِي	A collection of the traditions of the Prophet by Imam Darimi.
SUNAN, AN-NASA'I	سُنَنُ النَّسَائِي	A collection of the traditions of the Prophet by Imam Nasa'i.
SUNAN, AT-TIRMIDHI	سُنَنُ التِرمِذِي	A collection of the traditions of the Prophet by Imam Tirmidhi.
SUNAN, IBN MAJA	سُنَنُ ابنُ مَاجَه	A collection of the traditions of the Prophet by Imam Ibn Maja.
SUNNA	سُنَّة	All the traditions and practices of the Prophet that have become as models to be followed by the Muslims.
SŪRA	سُورَة	A chapter of the Qur'an.
TĀ AL-MARBŪTA	تَاءُ الْمَرْبُوطَة	The feminine ending of nouns or adjectives; it is written as (ة).
TĀ AT-TĀNITH	تَاءُ التَّانِيث	Same as Tā al-Murbuta ة .
TĀ MUDAWWARA	تَاءٌ مُدَوَّرَة	The round ta; same as Tā al-Murbuta ة .
TĀ TAWĪLA	تَاءٌ طَوِيلَة	The ordinary tā ت .
TA'AWWUDH	تَعَوُّذ	To start the recitation of the Qur'an by saying: اَعُوذُ بِاللهِ مِنَ الشَّيطٰنِ الرَّجِيم "I seek God's protection from Satan, the rejected one."
TADWĪR	تَدوِير	A method of recitation between labored recitation of Tartīl اَلتَّرتِيل and hurried recitation of Hadr اَلحَدر .
TAFKHĪM	تَفْخِيم	Thick or heavy pronunciation.

TAFSĪR	تَفْسِير	A commentary; exegis; a critical explanation of the Qur'anic verses.
TAHQĪQ	تَحْقِيق	Same as Tartīl; a method of recitation in slow, measured rhythmic tones.
TAJWĪD	تَجْوِيدْ	The art of recitation of the Qur'an.
TANWĪN	تَنْوِين	Nunation; sound of the letter nūn; double fatha (ً), double ḍamma (ٌ), and double kasra (ٍ).
TANWĪN, DOUBLE ḌAMMA		See Tanwīn.
TANWĪN, DOUBLE FATHA		See Tanwīn.
TANWĪN, DOUBLE KASRA		See Tanwīn.
TARQĪQ	تَرْقِيق	Thin or soft pronunciation.
TARTĪB AN-NUZŪL	تَرْتِيبُ النُّزولِ	The order in which the verses of the Qur'an were revealed.
TARTĪB AT-TILĀWA	تَرْتِيبُ التِّلاَوَة	The arrangement of the Qur'an in book form as instructed by the Prophet.
TARTĪL	اَلتَّرْتِيل	A slow, measured rhythmic recitation of the Qur'an.
TASHDĪD	تَشْدِيد	When a consonant occurs twice, it is written once only and the sign (ّ) is place over it to be pronounced twice.
THALĀTHA	ثَلاَثَة	3/4 [of a Juz].
TILĀWA	تِلاَوَة	The recitation of the Qur'an.
'UBAYY BIN KA'B	اُبَيّ بِن كَعَب	A Companion of the Prophet, a famous reciter of the Qur'an and a scribe of the Prophet who is considered to have memorized the entire Qur'an during the lifetime of the Prophet.
'UMAR BIN AL-KHATTAB	عُمَرُ بِنِ الْخَطَّاب	Of all the Companions of the Prophet, he was the most intimate to him after Abu Bakr. He is highly regarded for the strength of his faith, firmness of his mind and his acute sense of justice. He was the second Rightly-Guided Caliph.

'UTHMAN BIN 'AFFAN	عُثْمَانُ بِن عَفَّان	One of the Close companions of the Prophet, his son-in-law and the third Rightly-Guided Caliph of Islam.
WUDU'	وُضُوء	Ablution; ritual cleanliness (washing of hands, face, and feet) required to offer the Prayers.
WĀJIB	وَاجِب	Lesser than Fard and greater than Sunna.
WAQF	وَقْف	A stop; refers to a complete stop, breaking the breath during the recitation of the Qur'an.
WAQF, AL-HASAN	وَقْفُ الْحَسَن	A type of voluntary stop during recitation at a point where the sentence is complete but the meaning is not.
WAQF, AL-KĀFĪ	وَقْفُ الْكَافِي	A type of voluntary stop during recitation at a point where sentence or a part of it is complete but something more follows.
WAQF, AL-MUTLAQ	وَقْفُ الْمُطْلَق	Denotes a full stop, i.e., the end of the sentence but not the end of an argument.
WAQF, AL-QABĪH	وَقْفُ الْقَبِيح	A stop during recitation where neither the sentence nor the meaning is complete; sometimes such a stop will change the meaning.
WAQF, AT-TĀMM	وَقْفُ التَّام	A stop indicating the end of a verse; indicated by a small circle.
WAQF, IKHTIBĀRĪ	وَقْفٌ اِختِبَارِي	Stopping to show how a waqf should be made at any word in a verse.
WAQF, IKHTIYĀRĪ	وَقْفٌ اِختِيَارِي	Stopping under control at the end of a complete sentence.
WAQF, INTIZĀRĪ	وَقْفٌ انْتِظَارِي	Stopping to show the variation in the recitation by one of the seven or ten recognized versions of the recitation of the Qur'an.
WAQF, IDTIRĀRĪ	وَقْفٌ اِضْطِرَارِي	An unintentional stopping due to running out of the breath, sudden cough, sneeze or other emergencies.
WAQF, LĀZIM	وَقْفٌ لَازِم	An absolutely necessary stop.
WAṢL	وَصْل	A continuous recitation without pause or stop.

WAṢL, HAMZA-TUL	هَمزَةُ الْوَصْل	A hamza at the beginning of certain verbs and nouns; it is not pronounced in continuous reading, e.g. Irtabu اِرتَابُو but Amir Tabu ام ارتَابُو in continuous reading.
ZAID BIN THABIT	زَيدُ بِن ثَابِت	A Companion and a scribe of the Prophet who is considered to have memorized the entire Qur'an during the Prophet's lifetime.
ZUBAIR IBN AL-AWWAM	زُبَيرُ ابِن الْعَوَّام	A Companion of the Prophet.

APPENDIX B
Glossary of Phonetic Terms

ALVEOLAR	Articulated with the tip of the tongue touching or near the teeth ridge.
ALVEOLUS	Relating to teeth ridge.
ALVEOLAR RIDGE	Teeth ridge.
ARTICULATION, POINT OF	The place from which a sound is articulated.
ARTICULATION	To utter clearly and distinctly; an act or manner of pronouncing sounds.
ARYTENOIDS	Relating to a pair of small muscles of the larynx to which the vocal cords are attached.
ASPIRATION	The act of breathing.
ASSIMILATION	Change of a sound in speech so that it becomes identical with a neighboring sound, e.g. in the word cupboard the /P/ sound of the word "cup" has undergone complete assimilation.
BILABIAL	A sound produced with both lips; relating to both lips.
EMPHATIC	A particular prominence given in reading or speaking to a particular sound; utter with emphasis.
EPIGLOTTIS	A thin plate of flexible cartilage in front of the glottis that folds back over and protects the glottis during swallowing.
FRICATIVE	Hissy sound produced when the letters such as s س , sh ش , etc. are pronounced.
GLOTTAL STOP	A term referring to the pronunciation of the letter hamza.
GLOTTIS	The elongated space between the vocal cords.
GUTTURAL	Relating to the throat, articulated in the throat.
HARD PALATE	Bony part of the roof of the mouth.
LABIAL	Relating to lips; uttered with the participation of one or both lips.
LABIO-DENTAL	Term referring to lips and teeth; uttered with the participation of the lips and teeth.
LARYNX	Upper part of the wind pipe.
NASAL	Relating to nose; uttered through the nose with the mouth passage closed.
NASAL CAVITY	Hollow space in the nose.

NASALIZED — A sound in which the oral passage is partially blocked and some of the air passes out through the nose and some through the mouth; to speak in a nasal manner.

NOSTRILS — Nose openings.

OESOPHAGUS — Food pipe; a muscular tube connecting mouth to the stomach.

ORAL — Relating to the mouth; uttered by the mouth.

ORAL CAVITY — Hollow space in the mouth.

PALATAL — Sound produced with the blade of the tongue near the hard palate.

PALATE, HARD — Bony part of the roof of the mouth.

PALATE, SOFT — Muscular part of the roof of the mouth located at the back (towards the throat).

PHARYNGEAL — Relating to the throat; uttered in the throat.

PHARYNX — The throat (it is a tube connecting the larynx with the mouth and the nose).

PHONETICS — Relating to spoken language or speech sounds.

PHONOLOGY — The science of speech sounds in a language.

PLOSIVE — A method to produce speech sound in which the flow of air in vocal tract is blocked by the tongue or lips, suddenly releasing the air pressure built up, as in sounds like b (ب) or j (ج), etc.

QUALITY — Peculiar and essential characteristic sound; the identifying character of a sound in uttering it.

SOFT PALATE — See palate, soft.

TEETH-RIDGE — The inner surface of the gums of the upper front teeth.

TRACHEA — Wind pipe; a tube connecting lungs to the mouth through which air passes.

TURBULENT — Characterized by agitation and disturbance.

UTTER — To pronounce; to speak.

UVULA — The fleshy lobe in the middle of the back of the soft plate.

UVULAR — Relating to uvula; sound produced with the aid of the uvula.

VELAR — Relating to soft palate; sound produced with the back of the tongue touching or near the soft palate, e.g. kaf (ك) or of qaf (ق).

VOCAL — Uttered with voice.

VOCAL CORDS — Cords in the vocal tract used to utter sound.

VOCAL TRACT — Air passage from the lungs to the lip.

SUGGESTED REFERENCES

Ahmad, I. *What Do the Muslims Owe to the Qur'an*. Lahore, Pakistan: Markazi Anjuman Khuddamu'l-Qur'an, 1973.

Ali, A. Y. *The Holy Qur'an, Translation and Commentary*. Beirut, Lebanon: Printing Publications, 1965.

Al-Ani, S. H. *Arabic Phonology: An Accoustical and Physiological Investigation*. The Hague: Mouton, 1970.

Bucaille, M. *Le Bible, Le Coran et Le Science*. Paris, France: Seghers Publishers, 1977.

Da'as, I. I. *Fun al-Tajwid*. Cairo, Egypt. Undated.

Eliasi, M. A. H. *The Holy Qur'an: Transliteration in Roman Script*. Hyderabad, India: Burney Academy of Islamic Studies, 1971.

Al-Ghazali, A. H. *Ihya 'Ulum ad-Din*. Beirut, Lebanon: Dar al-Ma'rifa, undated.

Hussain, S. M. *Qawa'id Tajwīd wa Qira'at: Mosum ba at-Tajwid*. Hyderabad, India: Madrasa Deenyat First Lancers, 1952.

Husaini, S.K. *Sahl Tajwid*, Hyderabad, India, Maktaba Darul Qiraat al-Kaleemiyah, 1977.

Iqbal, Z. *Tajwidi Qur'an*, Lahore, Pakistan: Packages Ltd., 1391 AH.

Islahi, A. A. *Tadabbur al-Qur'an*, Lahore, Pakistan: Faran Foundation, 1979.

Jung, N. *An Approach to the Study of the Qur'an*. Lahore, Pakistan: Sheikh Muhammad Ashraf, 1970.

Khalilullah, M. *Tajwidu'l-Qur'an*. Karachi, Pakistan: Urdu College, Undated.

Maududi, S. A. A. *The Meanings of the Qur'an*. Lahore, Pakistan: Islamic Publications Ltd., 1967.

'Othman, H. S. *Haqq-ut-Tilawah*. 'Amman, Jordan. Maktaba al-Manar, 1401 AH.

Al-Qadri, S. H. M. *Ataleeq Tajwidu'l-Qur'an*. Hyderabad, India: Saeed al-Madaris Publications, 1347 AH.

Quasem, M. A. *The recitation and Interpretation of the Qur'an*. London, England: Kegan Paul International, 1982.

Saiyyara Digest, Qur'an Number Vol. I, Lahore, Pakistan, 1968.

Saiyyara Digest, Qur'an Number Vol. II, Lahore, Pakistan, 1969.

Saiyyara Digest, Qur'an Number Vol. Ill, Lahore, Pakistan, 1970.

Saqr, A. B. *Al-Tajwid wa 'Ulumu'l-Qur'an*. Damascus, Syria: Manshoorat al-Maktabu'l-lslami, 1389 AH.

Semaan, K. I. *Linguistics in the Middle Ages: Phonetic Studies in Early Islam*. Atlantic Highlands, N.H.: Humanities Press, Inc., 1968.

Siddiqui, A. *Al-Qur'an: Guidance for Mankind*. The light of Islam, Lahore, Pakistan, 1966.

Sieny, Mohmoud E. *Qur'anic Arabic*. The MSA of the U.S. and Canada, Undated.

Simplified Rules of Tajweed. Johannesburg, South Africa: Waterval Islamic Institute, Undated.

Thatcher, G. W. *Arabic Grammar of the Written Language*. London, Great Britain: Lund Humphries and Co. Ltd., 1942.

Tritton, A. S. *Learn Arabic for English Speakers*. New York: Saphrograph Corporation, 1974.